Quarterly
Review of

EDITED BY T. & R. WEISS

Literature

Poetry Book Series
VOLUME XXXV

Lynne Knight
Dissolving Borders

Jean Hollander
Moondog

David Citino
The Weight of the Heart

Barbara D. Holender
Is This the Way to Athens?

Maria Banus
Across Bucharest After Rain
Translated from the Rumanian by Diana
Der-Hovanessian and Mary Mattfield

26 HASLET AVENUE, PRINCETON, NEW JERSEY 08540

ACKNOWLEDGEMENTS

MARIA BANUS: Some of these poems were published in *Kayak, Christian Science Monitor, Graham House Review, Visions* and *Die Young* and are reprinted with permission and thanks.

DAVID CITINO: I thank the editors of the following journals, where these poems were published originally, in some cases in slightly different form. *Agni:* "A Modern History of California." *The American Literary Review:* "Swastika," "Sister Mary Appassionata on the Cholesterol Levels of the Gods." *The Centennial Review:* "The Threat of Allergies in the Afterlife," "Senior Class Play: *A Man for All Seasons,*" "Bread," "With the Visiting Writer," "The Sorrow of What Flies," "Phil Ochs Is Dead." *The Chariton Review:* "Those Old Songs." *Cimarron Review:* "Sister Mary Appassionata to the Editor of *The Columbus Dispatch.*" *Colorado Review:* "U2 Concert, Cleveland Municipal Stadium." *Cream City Review:* "Bathing Lenin," "Walking by the Lion's Den Adult Theatre and Bookstore, Sister Mary Appassionata on the Nature of the Hero." *The Dalhousie Review:* "Sister Mary Appassionata Praises the Sense of Smell." *Kansas Quarterly:* "Three Versions Culminating in the Minimal." *Laurel Review:* "The Quantum Mechanics of Fathers and Sons," "*Name that Tune* in the Foro Romano," "The Meaning of April," "Sister Mary Appassionata on the Nature of the Hero." *The Literary Review:* "Egyptian Tomb Painting, Aztec Sacrifice, Central Ohio Autopsy." *Memphis State Review:* "Howard Carter Unwraps King Tut: Or, Curse of the Mummy's Tomb." *National Forum:* "Alabama Farmer Just Misses Being Last Casualty of Civil War." *New Letters:* "Illustration." *Nimrod:* "Loving the Stars," "The Nocturnal Migration of Songbirds." *ONTHEBUS:* "Labor Day." *The Ohio Poetry Review:* "The Betrayal of the Father," "Octopus." *The Pennsylvania Review:* "Possum." *Poetry:* "My Father Shaves with Occam's Razor." *Prairie Schooner:* "The Train into the Mountainside, the Miracle of the Bus." *Seneca Review:* "Dear Robert: I Dreamed That You Were Dead of AIDS, and Now You Are." *South Dakota Review:* "Daisy." *Southern Humanities Review:* "Bread for the Dead." *Southern Poetry Review:* "Ghost of Elvis Makes Love to Me: Now I Carry His Baby." *Tar River Poetry:* "Thefts from Italian Churches Reach All-Time High." *VIA: Voices in Italian Americana:* "NATO Airbase Proposed for Southern Italy." *West Branch:* "Vagrant Found Dead Near River."

BARBARA HOLENDER: The following poems have appeared in print: in *Helicon Nine:* "Straw Into Gold," "The Little Mermaid," "Collage"; in *The Literary Review:* "A Gift Of Galtonia Princeps"; in *The Kansas City Star:* "Even To Begin"; in *The New York Times:* "Among These Rocks"; in *Poet Lore:* "The Little Life"; in *Prairie Schooner:* "A Field Of Green Tables," "Cloud Cover," "A Geodetic View". In *The Diamond Anthology* (A.S.Barnes, 1974) "Among These Rocks"; in *80 On The 80's* (Ashland Poetry Press, 1990) "Happy Birthday Buckminster Fuller"; in *Lifecycles* (Jewish Lights, 1994) "Song For Her Next Age"; in *A Poem In A Pamphlet* (Andrew Mountain Press, 1985) "Bible Students In The Sukkah" (reprinted in *Sarah's Daughters Sing*, KTAV, 1990); in *Poetry Inspired By Art In The Albright-Knox* (Orchard, 1982) "Burchfield Paints A Birch Field"; in *Scarecrow Poetry: The Muse In Post-Middle Age* (Ashland Poetry Press, 1994) "Swimming Against The Tide"; in *Without A Single Answer* (Judah L. Magnes Museum, 1990) "The Tank".

JEAN HOLLANDER: Some of these poems first appeared in: *Poetry Digest, Southern Humanities Review, New Mexico Review, California State Poetry Quarterly, Calapooya Collage, Dalhousie Magazine, South Florida Review, Poet, Poet Lore, The Denny Poems, Rage Before Pardon* (an anthology), *Poets On: Arrivals, WPFW 89.3 FM Poetry Anthology, Without Haloes* (an anthology), *Poem Card, Parting Gifts, Lips, The Cresset, US1, Appalachia, Alms House Press, The Devil's Mill Hopper, Allen Ginsberg Poetry Awards, Confrontation, The Paterson Review1.* My thanks to the New Jersey State Council on the Arts for awarding me three poetry-writing fellowships, and to US 1 for their suggestions and support.

LYNNE KNIGHT: Grateful acknowledgment is made to the following journals in which some of these poems appeared.*The Beloit Poetry Journal:* "Clearing Acanthus," "Holding Patterns," "The Story"; *Berkeley Poetry Review:* "Possession"; *CQ:* "The Limits Between Us"; *Cream City Review:* "All We Intended," "Slides"; *The Gettysburg Review:* "Bedtime Story"; *Kansas Quarterly:* "Loss"; *New England Review:* "Dissolving Borders"; *Northwest Review:* "Hairpins," "Parallel Lines," "Remembering the Names"; *North Dakota Quarterly:* "Appropriate Lover," "Still Life as an Inexact Translation"; *Poetry:* "Her Story," "Not Even They Could Stop It, and They Were Myth"; *Poetry East:* "The Bodies of Lovers,; "Eighteen," "Empty Arms," "There, in My Grandfather's Old Green Buick"; *Poetry Flash:* "Lament"; *Poetry Northwest:* "And Afterwards, the Longing"; *Poets On:* "My Father's Ashes," "No Wonder I Want You"; *Prairie Schooner:* "The Argument Against Chaos," "The Child Is Mother of the Longing"; *Santa Clara Review:* "The Omen Seekers," "Some memories flash before us"; *Texas Review:* "Bright Combs." "Her Story" was reprinted in *Calyx* (vol. 15, no. 3). "There, in My Grandfather's Old Green Buick" was reprinted in *Drive, They Said* (Milkweed Editions, 1994).

Assistants: Bill Davis, Tyler Doggett, Michael Donohue,
Michael Emmerich, Steven Nardi
Designer: Mahlon Lovett
Cover Monotype: Roselyn Karol Ablow, *Passage*, 1995

For   Michael

LYNNE KNIGHT

Dissolving Borders

LYNNE KNIGHT was born in Philadelphia, Pennsylvania, but grew up in Cornwall-on-Hudson, New York. After graduating from the University of Michigan and Syracuse University, she lived in Canada for several years, where her daughter was born. She lived for many years in upstate New York. In June of 1990, she moved to Berkeley, California. Since then, her work has appeared in a number of journals, including *Beloit Poetry Journal*, *Gettysburg Review*, *Poetry*, and *Poetry Northwest*. She teaches English at two community colleges. *Dissolving Borders* is her first full-length collection.

CONTENTS

SECTION ONE

We walk through the aquarium's blue light
behind the father and child he holds
up to the tank like an offering,
and he keeps saying it wrong, *Anna moans,*
look, anna-moans, the child whispering
chorus until I see in the anemones
the face of my great-grandmother Anna,
whom I knew only from tintypes
found in a shoebox soft and damp to the touch
as flesh, found as a child in her
daughter's attic, where my mother had warned
me to stay with my dolls on the open patch
of planked floor, away from the strange
architecture of trunks and boxes. A shoebox
wouldn't matter, I thought, pulling it free,
and then the face I didn't know, grieved,
though I didn't know grieving, either.
Not that year, but soon, I heard
the story over and over, how her husband
had teamed the horses and taken off
across the Hudson on a January night
and plunged through the ice; horses, carriage,
all; and not till the thaw weeks later
did they find him, washed ashore below
Storm King. They poured whiskey down her
throat to stop the screams. And then the part
I thrilled to hear: *They buried her*
with him. She never said his name
again—her children's; anyone's. She never
spoke. But at night they'd hear her
in her room, moaning as a dog moans
at full moon. That was grief, then:
no words for it . . .

Now I stare at the anemones,
their reds and purples pulsing in a rhythm
like the heart's, seeing the cascade
of leather, wheel, blanket, horse; the wild
wheeling eyes of the man powerless to stop
plunging deeper into water, the cold
shock of it, the mute screams that carried
straight to her heart and stayed there
the rest of her life, opening at night
like these flowers I imagine I can hear
breathing under water . . .

The child whispers again. We move
on to the next tank, red-bellied piranhas
that hang like ornaments in the water, bright,
harmless. But if the glass were to break—.
He'd driven the river for years. Sometimes
she went with him, her dark hair streaming
in the wind, wild with it like the horses'
manes. The ice held them like the hand
of God, she wrote once in her diary. Or
someone who loved irony added that to what
I'm telling you now, making it up as I go,
by way of telling you all I keep being
unable to say, how losing you would feel
like losing the words to the story.

Who ends up telling it
matters as much as what's told:
Imagine Leda controlling her trembling

as the swan thrust deeper,
losing all sense of time
until she picked at a feather stuck to her thigh,

insisting *It was more*
like death than life. Dissolve to real
time, annihilated by the white sun, the white

man coming into the hut
while the woman lay in shadow, knowing
her screams would only mix in with the cicadas,

the crows, the words he would
deny like the coldness he could feel
trembling through her though she lay still, lay

still enough for death. I
have my own version, woke to it
one morning years ago, someone's hands

at my throat, my voice
through the cloth of the pillowcase
already hollow with what I was about to lose,

had already lost because
sleep had become a place violence
could invade with the dream's ease, the dream's

silence. I tried to tell
the story until it became someone
else's, until the hands at my throat dissolved

like a dream image,
fragment offering no clear
portent, the feather from the pillow

stuck to my brow afterwards
when I looked into the mirror and saw
another woman trembling to seize control.

BEDTIME STORY

Finding it hard to communicate,
they began to speak through
stuffed animals. *Ms. Bear would love
an evening without loud music*
or *Morgan thinks the pasta would taste
a little better with less hysteria.*
For a while the bear and gorilla
sufficed, but soon it was clear
they too had trouble mentioning
the delicate. Love, for example.
So two small rabbits appeared,
pink-eared, tender, contemplative.
They had high-pitched voices,
Elmer Fudd accents, anagrammatic
names. They were adorable. Things
became more tender and defined,
an interlude, and might have gone on
like that, but one day Morgan introduced
a hippopotamus. So much for interlude.
For one thing, M Hippo took up
an entire chair and insisted on speaking
in the most pedantic tone, like some
tight-buckled classics professor.

Worse, he used the regal plural.
We note and *We hesitate* and *We should like.*
After a few days of this, Ms. Bear
sat down at dinner one night
and refused to say anything but
What's with this asshole.
Morgan stared at the floor,
yawning, affecting restraint.
The rabbits imitated being caught
in a trap and made horrible
squealing noises. M Hippo
(pronounced in the Gallic way)
kept asking for more pasta,
but *without that abominable house sauce*
we believe you call hysteria.
Well, he got it right where.
There was shouting, breakage, a mess.
Then silence. The two-legged animals
going in and out with sponges, brooms,
resolute jaws of *The End.*

LAMENT

I took them all to forget you.
The first one liked to keep one step ahead
and what he said got lost in the rush
of traffic headed in the same direction
I took when I left. Then the one
who wanted me to read the news every
morning while he waited for the sun
to do something rare, something worthy
of poetry; incinerate me right
there in my chair, say. I left without
a word. The next one held my hair
like flame. I felt my face disappear.
And the one who picked the notes on his guitar
like fruit and left them for me to eat.
The one who said what they all said.
The one who spoke in things.
The one whose tongue went everywhere.
The one whose seed I swallowed like a pill.
And still the hollow in my heart,
the hollow echo in my ear.
The nights no dream could interrupt
dragging their blacks into day . . .
And still the hollow everywhere
when I cry your name.

do you think the sky, having
heard you, will lay its face
against the water and hold still
while all the air drains out?

Then everything would be no color.

Do you think the stones will empty
their veins in the night,
their cries mistaken for owls,
their blood for dawn?

Then nothing underfoot would be safe.

Do you think I have no room for you,
do you imagine having to grope your way
along the walls to the heart, hoping
for another loss to pull you in?

Then anything would sound like treason.

Little truth, little sadness,
you are too small to make an echo.

In the rubble of Sarajevo, you'd be
black dust rising in the night.

Blake's worm would eat you without moving.
The rose would let go its thorns.

Why, then, do I cry out like all the world?

All morning she lay in bed, reading
Edna O'Brien's *A Fanatic Heart,*
drinking tea long cooled,
thinking about her own fanatic heart,
how far she'd carried it from
her mother's womb. The room
had the lazy smell of summer,
her own heat, her lover's seed.
Outside, the sporadic thud
of apples dropping to the lawn
her neighbor, helping out because
her back was bad, had mowed toward dusk
the day before, starting at the far edge
just as she'd led her lover up to bed,
the neighbor guiding a steady stream
of smaller and smaller rectangles
around the house, the motor louder
than their cries until it seemed
it was their cries, their bodies one
machine, and then the silence, the sweet
mix of cut grass, sweat, her perfumed
hair. Sleep, talk, and then he'd left
for the life he'd been trying to leave,
the one that left him feeling faithless
to himself, or so he'd said again, his fingers
tracing slow lines and circles on the sheet,
her breasts, as if he were puzzling out
a problem of geometry, but aimlessly,
like someone who'd forgotten something
crucial, numbers or the alphabet.

She thought of it like that: a problem
of geometry, and so she thinks again,
setting the book back on the shelf,
stretching like her mother at the end

of ironing, mending, some task a woman never
could feel easy leaving, her mother said,
knowing it would begin again. A burst
of apples, loosened by the quarrel of two
squirrels, the whir of a more distant mower
through the screen: and now she can no longer elude
the sadness she's resisted all these hours.
His fingers had stopped abruptly, like
a pencil breaking off, and then he'd stood
to pull his clothes back on, his skin like
marble in the dark; marble, stone, something
cold and unanswerable. She'd held still, felt
her own fingers begin where his left off,
tracing a pattern on the sheet, smaller
and smaller, fanatic for order,
resolution, some equivalent to faith.

He dreamed of open graves.
Sometimes the mouth of a woman
spoke with his own tongue
of going deeper, not so much
into her as beyond: green bank
of a river in the sun and no way
of knowing how many bones
had longed for comfort there.
Because the bones could long.
Some days he'll be standing at the window
or walking where he always walks
and feel his body want
to pull beyond him, as if
the skin were mere transparency
and all it held (he thinks of bones
and blood) could gather
where it willed. The dead
he mourns: brother, grandmother,
grandfather; suicides he reads of
in the paper; the war dead
(his father's eyes when he returned).
Women who said *I can't help it,
it just feels dead.* Women who said
nothing, but composed careful letters.
Sometimes the mouth of a woman
speaks with his own tongue
of going deeper. Sometimes it's his own
mouth, a busy corner, that wide open
earnest not to stop
until he's learned what's hidden
in the shadows of his bones.

DEVOTIONS, SIX O'CLOCK

after Paul Klee's La Belle Jardinière

The beautiful gardener stood in the rain
and sang down to the roots
of all she'd lost and seen returned.
Her blue skirt darkened
like the patch of sky gone black
an hour back in warning.
Her shirt clung to her breasts,
thin hair to her skull.
Everything was hers: both joy and threat.
She thought of lovers, all
of them lost or gone, how the taste
of the body was like rain: nothing
you could name, just that mix
of sweet and steel in the hollow
of the tongue. She sang down
to the vein until the lovers
rose before her, ghostly
in the wet and steel-bright light.
It was not madness.
She studied their faded eyes,
black shoes, the hands she would know
anywhere. What could she want from them,
they seemed to ask (each mouth
open like a bird's at dawn).
What had they still not given.
This devotion, she whispered.
And took their hands and danced
while rain came down and time bled
into everything withheld.

LOSS

One night you find yourself standing alone
at the window you've looked through
for years, watching the water
in the bay seem not to move, thinking
how long it takes to comprehend
a life, even when it's your own,
because it's so easy to confuse
one word with another when water
keeps moving and anyone might walk
into your arms yet still seem distant,
not like the stars or rivers
you remember naming as a child
but your hands, open, seeming
too small for all but the most minor
history even though you recall love
and disaster falling into them . . .
So you stand there with everything
mixing together until there's nothing
to do but stop yourself from feeling
that mouth again, that hand,
that body beside you moving
off like water in the night.

> *Each woman, lost in her reflection.* . .
> —Simone de Beauvoir

1.
No sense relying on palm line, bone,
streaks in hair, striation
of stone or eye,

no, all such signals contravene what must
be understood, these faces
in the mirror in

the pink-tiled room this noon, com-
posing themselves despite
how life's going

too fast to read every line of, I can
tell by the way their eyes
won't stop and the

way we're all leaning closer,
as if we might call things
into reverse,

as if that were all there was to it.

2.
She doesn't want much. Just to breathe,
she says. The mother hunched
by the crib, the girl

in the backseat feeling her jeans unzip,
the woman too frightened by dark
to walk anywhere but down

the center of the street, the lover burying her
face in his shirt for hint of betrayal—
none of them want all

the available air, just enough to endure.
Is that really so much to ask?
she says, turning

with wet hands for a towel, pressing
her lips together until her
mouth disappears,

as if that were all there is to it.

3.
Eyelash on forearm, torn hem, stall
door slamming shut on a word,
the same word on more

than one tongue—all of us thinking back
through our mothers, their mothers,
who taught what to look for,

how to read what life's got in store
the way we read faces in mirrors,
deciphering signs

of the war against time, powder and dye,
hollow and curve, but even then
something missing, the hollow

spiraling up from the heart staring us down,
Mirror, mirror, and the mouth always
empty, the glass slipper so small

not even a tongue would fit into it.

4.
Raven and owl, cracked crystal, spilled salt.
We know what we know. After one year,
two, the beloved caught in a yawn.

Hollow of a different order. The heart fades
faster than skin, than stars, black dust
surrounds us, we're done for.

Shades of that night he sat watching the sky,
all talk exhausted, white roses so heavy
they drooped past the mouth of

the vase, mute surrender I thought
my survival hung on learning
to replicate, eyes shut.

But at some point things stop meaning what they meant.

5.
All that time spent waiting for
the shoe to fit, for the shoe
to drop, for the voices

that scratch past the black at the back
to stop saying it over and over—
Mirror, mirror . . .

But we've had it with echoes, we've had it
with promises rubbing against us
like nails in our shoes,

we've had it with portents of doom. We may look like
no more than obedient moons, waiting for light
to reflect, but that's no more

than illusion: We're turning to seek what there is.

REMEMBERING THE NAMES

Once everything seemed clear
without eyeglasses or history.
You could tell from the way you held your cup
how heavy your heart had grown during a night
when sleep kept standing you up like the one
you'd have given anything to have again
until you did, and then longing shifted
like the stars in another hemisphere,
making you wonder if you'd ever find
your way back to the time when seeing
a woman lift her hair from her neck
for your mouth to move there
was enough, you could bear anything
for such a clear gesture, not that
belief required an offer so tactile,
not even that you required belief. But
something to stop you from looking
up at the sky and remembering the names
of all the constellations, night
after night, as if saying them
could redeem the idea of loss,
as if longing could occur
in the simple sound of a name.

APPROPRIATE LOVER

What if a lover comes to you
on a motorcycle, what little hair
that's left matted by his helmet
to his skull, his thick boots
marking up the kitchen floor,
the flowers you'd imagined held in wooing
still holding fast to blues and purples
along the country road you live on

because the city and its noise
take you too near the voices saying
Oh, sweetie, isn't it time to be practical?

What if the only language he speaks well
is the language of your body,
what if your most elaborate syntactical
connections break apart
under the touch of his wide hands
that have labored fields and machines,
are rough and stained, not at all
the hands you've imagined holding your breasts
in the light of an afternoon
when the heat will make your bodies
swim against the currents of each other
until you find quick passage
into depths where words are laughter?

And what if the same voices tell you
you're too old to be heeding the cries
and bleatings of sex, what if all the while
they think you're smiling surrender
you're remembering the way he turned you
in the air until your body turned
to everything you knew was there within,
fish and flower and woods-deep animal?

All day, jays in the scrub oaks
flash their metallic blue.
Enough, that the body take on
some semblance of that sheen,
glow as it's learned to do
from star, moon, sea—
speak in blood and bone.

BRIGHT COMBS

In Jim's painting of the chickens
the air smells of jasmine
and the sky sinks deep enough to reach
China, which the chickens' delicate
bright feet will never touch.
But Jim's seen to that, let the Orient
enter through their combs,
their feathers white like geishas' skin,
the strange music their thin necks
flick into Nan's room
where Jim's painting hangs.

In Nan's room where Jim's painting hangs
and late afternoon light drifts
through the odor of jasmine,
we talk of how we long to find
direction, dig down
through the years until we come
to where we lost sight
of ourselves behind bright combs
or powders, behind the names
we let steal our own,
ignoring their jarring music.

The chickens hold still
in themselves. A signal
there, a way of beginning
the descent for the original.

Say it begins the way seas begin,
edged with light. Begins with the intent
to spare grief, sorrow, harm.
To protect, even. To keep the one hearing
safe like an animal deep in its shell.

But the edge, the sea, the light
receding like the past
though you know exactly
where you left it, where you can return.

As if truth were a place.
As if finding it were nothing more than
finding the edge, the demarcation,
and standing there like a child
anxious not to be the last chosen.

The faith required.
The same that allows you
to believe that light is radiant
energy, despite what happens
when you stare down through the water.

Say, then, it is loving more
than the simpler truth. Is moving
into the water with both hands closed
against cold or current.

But the hardness of it.
Of the catching or being caught.
Everything drifting in
thick, wet, dragging

you with it. Down and down.
And your hand like the hand
of someone else, reaching out.

Is this what is meant by forgiveness?
This nothing left to say?

ALL LOSS IS VISIBLE

My phantom this, my phantom that.
My pouch of eggs leaking out
a thousand a month:
my adored unborn.
O woman, woman, we are mouth
and mouth, we are slit
and cave, we are all about
opening.
So the next time he says
I can't do this anymore
rub his sorry back
with scented fingers
and pack him food for the road—
seeds he can tongue
all he wants—
till oceans run like rivers
and mountains rub their shoulders
on the moon.
No matter what, the seeds
won't know to open.
But you'll keep watch,
eye he can't close.

In the haze of a Bali morning, a man
washes the bones of his beloved.
Her skull gleams, he keeps dipping
his hand into a blue bucket,
letting water roll from his fingers
into the eye sockets, as if to quicken
whatever dreams have stilled there
during her long sojourn in the earth.
Now he will fit her bones together, ease
the shrouded bundle into a bright coffin,
bear her to the ceremony of cremation.

Those nights when my lover reached to soothe me
to sleep, soft pads of his fingers swirling
on my eyelids, no sound but that dry sound
and our breathing—. And one night,
toward the end, the first rain
after months of drought, coming
in bursts, as we had earlier. Then
a downpour closing in until the room
seemed narrow as a grave. I drowsed off
after him. If someone had asked me then

I would have sworn there were no signs
the end was near: I loved him, he was all.
But now as I watch the smoke swirl up
from the Balinese skull, I see
that when I opened my eyes later that night
and mistook a swirling of moonlit clouds
for fire about to tear through us,
I was dreaming of love so consuming
neither lover would know, at the parting,
whether it was the dead or the living
letting go.

A FABLE IN FRAGMENTS

The older woman becomes invisible.

A room, turned to shadow.
Whose?
Not the man who loved smiles,
the one who wanted to trade his round felt hat
for the young woman's smile.
Not the young woman I know
I was but whose skin I cannot remember,
no, now I am old, the man
gives me no more heed than he would
a shadow, and he's tired of shadows,
they press at his eyes
until he cries, unmoving, miracle
of the weeping statue;
they rattle down small chutes
of his ears like torn papers, vows;
only a saint might withstand
such intrusion and he's no saint,
just a poet.
Who so loves women he prays every night
for a woman whose arms he can die in,
young woman whose smile will force death
to crawl a few yards away, abject
animal under the porch
while the forest comes nearer with moonlight.
So death there on its haunches,
gnawing at fleas,
while he and the young woman caress,
a tenderness like spring leaves
though he will be more intent
on watching deer

border the clearing,
munching low tips of aspen.
Then the pained *Ah!*—
remembering all the breasts
he has nuzzled—while death whines on
and the young woman stares past the man
to the years ahead, her smile
so stunned with gloom he forgives her,
pulls all the shadows into
his eyes, she's amazed how
still he keeps while tears
bead the web his skin has become.
Too amazed to remember the room disappearing.
Nothing, then, but the deer, the moon,
the clearing as you have imagined it.

At this moment, thousands
are writing poems, lost to all but words
while the bills collect, the lover
broods, the child whines at the door,
the American door behind which
American poets are writing of moments
in China while Chinese poets are writing
of moments like doors, and just-starting-out
poets are writing of death,
of love,
but mostly of death,
and women poets are writing of sex,
their bodies their own
and hot, hot as their whispers will be later on
with the lover who no longer broods,
who has written a poem of his own, maybe,
or done something equally fine—
fought crime, taught math, examined
microbes or defendants—
and who's standing at the window
saying *God, that sunset,*
what color would you call the sky?
so that the poet, reluctant to ignore
anything rhetorical, tries:
violet, salmon, charcoal.
A possible sky, but not *the* sky.
Not even close, the lover says.
But kindly, tenderly, knowing it's exhausting
to find the right word
when the thing keeps changing
by the moment, and is never the same
in America as it is in China,
in love as it is in death.

The prison of memory, all these people moving freely
through the prison of memory, their faces all

wrong, like clocks with different times, because memory
takes time into its hands like water, don't think I can't

hear you whispering *Why hands, don't you think I have
enough*
to hold . . . but even stones in your memory have them,

hands, your own, acting as if no burden is beyond them,
oh, it could go on forever, this martyrdom of the *If only,*

with people walking free of guilt for as long as it takes to
ascend and descend "the irregular black staircases" of notes

in Chopin's first étude for as long as it takes those of us
who are not musicians to drink a beer or walk the dog for as

long as it takes sky to become blood-stricken if excess is
what you clamor after. Don't think I can't hear you trying

not to need me, need anyone, moving off with the quiet at the
backs of planets. The backs of eyes. Of notes. What if you

put on your coat now, the fabric stiff as stairs, and walked
into the night hoping darkness would pass for amnesia, what

if all the ones who've loved you opened their arms as you
neared and you heard the sound of water slipping from your

hands, you heard memory reversing this into music you knew
you could never elude. Would you stare like an animal

through its cold bars, your eyes looking neither out nor
in? Would you leave me again, knowing all it took you?

It's not physical.
Just because gravity's pulling
my skin like old fruit, don't think

this is all about
losing my looks because it's not
physical though there is a room, real as any

I've been in, narrow,
low-ceilinged, whose blank walls
invite some extremity. *Open a window,*

I think, hearing *Open a vein.*
Not that violence could occur here.
The room's serene; breathe too hard and the ricepaper

shades will tear. Breathe
too hard and the pain will rush back
like a lover who's left something crucial

behind, glasses, a hard
disk, keys. So there's nothing
to do but hold still and pray the heart won't dry

like an eye, like
a bone, did I hear someone whispering
crone. No, the room's empty, even the space

below the piano breathes
with nothing but shadows breathing
as light leaves and I long for soothing,

music in the shape of rain making
its way down the windows making the glass
translucent so I can breathe as hard as I please

and no one will hear me trying
to behave as if the room's wholly imagined
as if loss were nothing you could open the door and admit

FAILED LULLABY

Not even the wind
is unburdened.
In the lightness
of dust and seed, leaf,
tumbleweed, there is still
the weighing-down
by obligation.

Walking the streets at noon,
you see little sign of the grief
others carry. But this one
lost a father: dust.
This one lost a lover: seed.
This one's dream is gone
or out of reach.

You'd lift them free
if you could: wind.
And the bodies hunching forward,
the hat blown off and crushed
are the songs
your mother sang you
when your cries refused to hush.

SECTION TWO

When the first daughter was born,
the mother began the stories.
There was no time to waste.
Each one beating forward like the heart.
Each with more history than the last.
Then the second daughter.
Exhaustion, in the repetition.
In the second daughter's refusal
to take *The End* for the end.
Again she cried. The mother tried
singing, other languages,
mixing of plots
while the first daughter
lay in her bed, small quilt, small pillow,
thinking of the poison in the apple,
the wolf's wide mouth.

But nothing so terrible happened.
Soon both daughters turned to their own stories.
Thinking for years they were original.
Whispering the worst parts, oh,
the importance!
Then, themselves mothers, the night
they turned back the child's bed and felt
the small bed of memory,
not even needing the book in their hands then
because the low voice beat on
like their mother's—there by instinct,
you might say blood—at any rate
the means of passage:
and the child looking on amazed
that it was all so familiar,
long ago named.

SOME MEMORIES FLASH BEFORE US, LIKE THAT

summer afternoon with slow heat moving in
through open windows, slow as the white
curtains shifting in a breeze that did nothing
but offer empty promises, my mother said,
in that way she had of speaking to someone
just beyond me, though we were the only ones
there, side by side on the old silk sofa,
its pale stripes uneven with loose threads.
She'd just brought me a glass of lemonade,
fresh, a hint of sugar, and I held it still
until small bits of lemon pulp moored
along the ice chips. Don't gulp, she'd warned,
and added that about the breeze, and then resumed
her reading. A few bits of pulp had the shape
of teardrops, or the shape that teardrops had
in books my mother read me. So there would be
sadness in anything we did, I understood,
not in words but in the way my mother
sat beside me with her book while heat moved
in through open windows and cold started
moving up my fingers, on up in.

FIVE WHITE SHIRTS

What begins as longing continues
like these impatiens out the window,
wood pale at the stem with winter
and the reach for sun, so that whenever
I look out at them I'm not here at all

but in the woods between the house
and the old haybarn, the brook gone
loud with coming spring, the trees

bent low with cold as I am, newly thin
from having sworn off sweets for Lent.
I love the way hunger aches all the way in,

the way my jeans, rolled up to show
the red plaid flannel lining,
hang so free of me they might be hanging
from the clothesline in the oak grove
over there across the shale heap

where my mother's just unpinned
my father's oxford shirts,
five white shirts stiffened by March wind
until she has to pull them in like
sails. I don't let on I see her.
Tomorrow afternoon she'll iron them

downstairs in the cold unfinished house
while I dream through another book
or walk here to the brook to dream
a different life. I won't let on
I see her look at me as if she's

young again, her chafed hands clear,
her body bending not to lift the next
shirt from the basket but a spray
of trillium or violets she'll pin
above a girlish ear. I won't let on
I've sworn to be unlike her, find a man

who won't need drink to keep the nights
from yearning into morning as these trees
yearn into light. Sworn to have a house
with walls and carpets, curtained rooms.
Sworn not to live pretending

none of this is happening to me.
But the least thing, like the sight
of this impatiens, takes me back. I
stand in those woods, dreaming while
my mother hauls the last shirt in.
My hands go cold. I ache to be forgiven.

CHARADES

An unfinished house, mid-winter.
A father, drawing hallways, stairs,
thick-walled rooms on a yellow legal pad.
Long past dark, and mid-week:
measured shots of whiskey.

The mother's reading.
Closest to the oilstove.
Two flannel shirts, two pairs of socks.
The pages lift and fall.
Her eyelids beat like moths.

The older daughter sits between them,
chemistry notebook open on her lap,
elaborating doodles made in class.
Her lips move to the music in her head.
Tap tap goes her foot on the hard dirt floor.

The younger one does nothing but stare
at old quilts nailed to the rafters
to trap the heat. She's inside
a wagon, crossing high mountains.
No. A small boat, the high seas.

Hold on cries the night.

THERE, IN MY GRANDFATHER'S
OLD GREEN BUICK

He was touching me where no one
had touched me before, there,
in my grandfather's old green Buick
that wouldn't go in reverse,
so all the while I was worrying
how he'd get the car turned around
and headed back to his school,
there as we were under the dark pines
and his whispering, *Some day we'll be able*
to have each other completely, which thrilled me
even more than the touching though I knew
it was too formal for real passion, real passion
made you say things the nuns swore would damn
your soul, and what if they could see me now,
with my hair falling down and my lips
kissed raw and this prep school boy's hand
there, and there, and my heart knocking
the way it should have when the priest rang
the bells at Mass, and the Buick so wide
I worried he'd scrape the paint against the pines
and then he whispered *We have to stop Do you know why*
we have to stop and I nodded, thinking he meant
curfew, so I sat up and felt along the cloth
seat for my hairpins and redid my French twist
and nothing happened, he swung the Buick around
and we slipped past the pines with our headlights
still out and when we got there, I slid
behind the wheel and drove down the mountain
knowing something had happened I couldn't reverse
anymore than I could the Buick, knowing I wanted it,
no matter what the nuns said, I wanted it, I could feel
my body wet and alive as if there had been a birth.

EIGHTEEN

My father was driving over Storm King,
the old highway, carved into the side
of the mountain, sudden curves,
so he had to stare straight ahead
but would have anyway because he was talking
about passion, by which he meant
sex, sex being a word he couldn't say
in reference to me and my boyfriend, to whom
he objected because I'd had sex with him
and written home about it, a long rhapsodic
letter on the loss of my virginity, a shorter
version of which I'd typed out for my grandmother
who wrote back saying my grandfather, two years
dead, would probably have recommended waiting.
My father was telling me passion wouldn't last,
even when passion was good it only lasted
a couple of years, I shouldn't be confusing it
with love and deciding to drop out of school,
run off to Mexico, write novels and screw,
a word he could say, to make me hear
his despair, and all this time I was thinking
What does he know, what does he know,
looking down at my hands
that had been everywhere on my lover,
looking over at my father's hands
that once had held the whole of me,
had moved all over my mother,
What does he know, his hands and mine
both freckled, tensed—
so much tenderness lost
in fear of loss.

SHOULDN'T

. . . lift the rock and poke
the pale worms coiled there
until they thin and break like roots
while your mother's calling and calling

. . . ride your bike down River Road
where Daddy Longlegs lurks behind his
windblown door, ready to spin out from the dark
and grab hold while your mother's calling and calling

. . . tell what the older boys made you do
far back in the hayloft as rough warm hands
moved up your legs and you stared at sunbeams thick
with dust and they mocked your mother, calling and calling

. . . remember the pain of your father's being
so drunk he poured salt past his plate, long cold,
and folded butter in his bread while you watched the lost
look in your mother's eyes, like someone calling and calling

THE ARGUMENT AGAINST CHAOS

Pain was only a feeling.
Your mind shamed it,
made it slink off like an animal
caught stealing food.
Meanwhile the universe advanced
its argument against chaos.
The tides obeyed, the pelicans
flew in formation, the sun burned
through morning mist.
I brought you the newspaper,
dry in its plastic tube,

and the world continued,
the pelicans swooped in a row
to skim the waves for food,
the sun made the sea a mosaic.
The woman with dog walked by,
the red Ford pickup arrived;
its driver, wreathed by his net,
waded in for mullet.
I dumped orange rinds and egg shells
into the newspaper tube and took it down
to the garbage. When I came back up the steps
I looked in at you through the sliding glass door
and understood that pain had a face.
Then, weeks later, a sound.
I cannot shut the sound from my mind.
I want to believe it is the sound of a man
fighting chaos but it is animal
and terrible and eats
the air around it, it spares nothing,
it invades even blood.

LIGHT

The undertaker's stretcher seemed
too plain to bear the body of my father
into the predawn dark. I wanted him
laid the whole length of an oak canoe,
carried to the ocean's edge, let go.

Then it was day.
We did what people do.
Wept, ate what the neighbors brought,
said things about the merciful end.
Waited for the appointed hour
when we would drive into town
for his ashes.

My mother had nursed him for weeks.
Her arms ached from rolling and holding him
so she could pull the soiled sheets free.
She pulled at the air as she told this.
Then she cried out. In grief,
we thought. But heard the cry
was more a child's cry of fear:
My eye! I can't see! A great star

exploding in the far corner
of her eye, streaking in.
As if my father were sending a sign, or God were.
We had to shout her into a dress, the car.
It was only a floater, the doctor said,
from the strain she'd been under.

That night, when we were calmer
with wine and hours of her seeing clearly,
we sat staring out at the ocean. The last light
moved on it like something palpable. Like sheets,
lightly wrinkled, that someone kept trying to smooth.

The next day, or the next, as if time had rolled
back, my mother said without prelude
that towards the end she'd changed the sheets
three or four times a day.
The beach house had no washing machine,
so she did them by hand.
They took a long time to dry in the salt air.
She hung them under the house, among the stilts.
I could see her there, staring out at the ocean
to compose herself before going back up to him,
smoothing each sheet on her way.

So thin!

They never said it aloud, that he was dying.
It wasn't denial. It was more an embrace
of the last light they had to go by.

MY FATHER'S ASHES

I thought they'd weigh no heavier
on my hands than those of leaves
or old news vanishing up the woodstove

I thought they'd lift like flakes of skin,
only darker, forgetting about the bones,
how the fires would grind them down

I thought I'd pour them out like salt
straight down into the channel
to the ocean, not knowing how they'd swell

and thin like a cloud in sharp wind
or the noise of my mother weeping,
the long noise between death and farewell

I expected grief everywhere, visible,
dust settling on table and floor,
mixing in with more until its source

disappeared   But nine years this October,
and still the ashes, palpable, here
in my hands, the dense particular

weight of them, undefined as the roots
a gardener stoops to loosen,
her fingers numbing with cold

BLACK RIBBON

Dusting the
bedside table
I saw, half hidden
under stubs and
coupons, the black
ribbon he'd worn
to mourn his sister,
torn cloth pinned
to his shirt by
his heart for one
month to signify
how anger tore
through grieving.
On the day of
the burial
her husband
and sons had stood
while the rabbi
tore their shirts,
their own hands
hard at their sides.
I remembered
the morning
my father died,
how my mother's
hands had moved
near her heart
as if they had life
of their own,
were small
animals gnawing
there, making her
moan from the

pain. The ribbon
curled at the edge,
I blew on it
and dust drifted off
as my father's ashes
had drifted down
to the water,
as the ribbon
would drift
through wind
toward the bay.
But I laid
the ribbon back
where he meant it
to be—where he
no longer
needed it
now that grief
had found its way,
black ribbon
through the veins.

STILL LIFE AS AN INEXACT TRANSLATION

The Cézanne still life near my desk
holds a knife, a clean glass, a napkin
tossed back like a sheet, a milk tin,
apples someone must have just let rumble
from a sack though the napkin belies this—
whoever was there stood up, rushed out.

I thought of this last night while I tried to sleep
on my side of the bed as if nothing had changed,

you were still beside me, not thousands of miles
away mourning your sister, whose death
had so magnified space each room in her house
seemed to keep emptying. When your sister's fingers
first felt the lump, there must have been
that same falling away of the familiar.

Some nights when you hold me as we fall asleep,
I feel the world fall away with the quiet of apples
being peeled into red or gold unbroken spirals
like those we watched fall toward white plates
at the outdoor cafe in Aix, not far from the house
where Cézanne, still a boy, stared at fruits
on the table, turning each piece slowly in his mind
until he could imagine letting it fall
into a coat pocket. Then, himself turning
to run outside into the shadows of plane trees
cooling the Cours Mirabeau, the intuition:
a thing's shadow extends and empties it.

I lay awake all night, or half-awake,
longing for you to be there, not turning
in whatever bed you turned in, your sorrow
so extreme you longed to leave your body
for a while. It seemed like such a simple thing
to ask for: a meal of bread, milk, fruit.
But there was nothing but the sheet,
thrown back like Cézanne's napkin
as if there'd been a sudden interruption—

One way of resolving the problem of loss
implicit in all paintings is to take
each color or shape one by one:
blue, gold, milk tin, fruit
and wait until the idea
of being able to touch it
empties from your hand.

THE BODIES OF LOVERS

When we think of the bodies
of our lovers, we think of the time
it took to know our own
enough to move free
inside a lover's arms,
of how the branches of trees
remind us every spring, when
their blossoms drift like lace
at the window, how strict a balance
loving requires—the slow loss
of self, as if we were no more
than those trees in the dark
orchards where we would sit past dusk
dreaming the dreams of girls, our tongues
hungry for the words lovers would whisper
over and over; and then the slower
acquiring, that one that began
when we rose and ran wordlessly home
along paths through the small woods
so familiar we knew every stone,
ran past our fathers, drunk or asleep
on the couch, ran up to our rooms
where we stood staring at the mirror
while we brushed our hair free
of twig or leaf, whispering our names
over and over, with the hunger
a lover would need.

1

While the male tortoise swims
through the shallows, the female
hauls herself ashore
to lay her eggs,
the ancient code telling her
Here. This sand. Eggs
black as the undreamed.
Her front legs finish the burial,
familiar sweeping gesture.

2

My mother and sister stared down
at the dirt floor. Now that the loan
had been refused, the house
would never be finished.
A big bird cage, the bankers said.
My father was upstairs, sober, smoking.
Each time he struck a match
I heard the gasp of someone weeping.
But when I crept upstairs to look,
he stood calm by the window.
Another scheme, my mother whispered.

3

You come from a long line of dreamers
my father says in the dream
where the house is finished with
all the wrong windows, doors
where doors were never intended.
I know this, know he's dead,
but nothing changes the way
I can look in any window and see him,
my mother, the long line

grief makes in its descent
from the back of the eyes
to the interior where
one dreamer yields another.

4

In the aridity of the Galapagos,
only those tortoises with necks long enough
to reach the leaves of cactus

survived. The short-necked
scrabbled from rock to muck, longing.
But never enough. Natural selection:
nothing for dreamers.

5

The optometrist holds the light by my eye.
Look up, he says.
My eyes are drugged, the windows
wide open, and if I keep still,
he tells me, I'll see what's always there
though my brain chooses to hide it—
blood vessels, the interior:
Purkinje's images.
I keep still.
A smooth surface, red clay
in a riverbed. Then a greenish
rush of veins, curved, thin;
design that intervenes
between waking and dreaming.

6

Everywhere, evidence of dreaming.
The boundless *if*, into which pour
cries from Plato's cave, hooftaps
of the conqueror's horse,
trampled crops, dust and thirst.

Repeat. Then hangman's noose,
assassin's knife, the wild reel
the dead begin while weapons rust.
Cries of pity, cries of woe—
but cries of joy are interspersed.
In the archives of the earth
bones turn to stone.
And, here and there, fossils
of land-living animals
that fell into water.
Watery feel of the fall into dreaming.

7

In the dream where we fall and fall
we learn the slow falling-away
of the body: cancer eating to the bone
until my father's eyes seemed orbs
left spinning where his face had been,
my mother going deaf to roars
so violent she dreams of fire.
I hear her at night far off in Florida,
dragged from one dream to the next,
her small arms brushing the sheets
as if she could reach the nearby sea
where we poured my father's ashes.
I want to die while I know who I am
she told me. And I knew that the cry
in my throat—*Don't leave me*—
went all the way back, coded
in layers of rock, dug into sand
like those eggs in the beginning,
sun-warmed and safe enough,
if it weren't for
the snake moving closer,
dark shapes at the shoreline,
the loved face in the window
receding from the dreamer's call.

Enough of blaze, of incandesce.
Bring on the winds, cold-tongued,
cold-fingered, to bite and snap
the last leaves off.

Then, when dull November
recites its lessons on
brevity, on loss, I'll pretend
the soul can be stripped bare

like oak or maple, year after year.
What grief I know will swirl down
to blur with general grief,
wind-swept, swept off.

I'll think of you less and less—
skeletal trace behind the eye
when it closes—barely
there—like a leaf, long-pressed.

For my father, dead in October

MY MOTHER (*Giving Me the Oriental Bowl*):

It's bone china, so thin toward the edge
I always think of eyelids.
Look at the branches, faint
blue, as if spring sky
had hardened into glaze.

The blossoms are only ideas.
No doubt a beginner painted them,
no older than my father when
he and an uncle toured the Orient,
much of it a blur

from boats they took upriver.
My father used to say the bowl
could take him back there.
Once I watched him stare down
as if to turn the water and its roses

into oracle. It was late summer,
the heat trapped by the room's dark wood.
We'd just come back from burying my brother.
If my father'd wept, I hadn't seen it.
I thought I'd see it then—the bowl so delicate,

those branches and their not-quite blooms.
I waited, shadowed by the doorway.
But he only stirred
the water with a finger.
They were tea roses,

cut from my mother's garden that morning.
He stirred again. I saw boats on the river,
their white sails packed like petals,
the blur of riverbank and figure,
the shimmer as things pass.

VISIT TO GIVERNY

White Peonies

Now I know that those nights
I lay waiting for sleep,
I was praying for my grief to turn white
as the white peonies
in this garden, resting
their heavy hearts
against the wet grass.

Chrysanthemums

This is why the stories
with chrysanthemums in the title
stay with me: The flowers are rigid,
they do not yield to the touch
as I expect. It must be the dead
flowing through them like fluid, tingeing
even the whitest blue, it must be you
flowing through them, wooing them
to bend to your claim.

Delphinium

Earlier this morning, the blue torches
rose through mist,
leading the way toward death.
What matter that no one was here to follow?
Each flower has enough blue flame
to burn through all denial.

Red Poppies

If I could lay my grief down.
If I could walk into a room
where a band played, let

my bright skirt flare,
if I could let go like that,
what joy would I not feel, shouting
through everything, even the trumpets.

Climbing Rose

Almost like a cloud caught on the trellis—
soft, beyond the material.
When the scale ascends, the heart stirs with hope.
But the gardener who sweeps the path clear
of petals every morning works quickly,
thinking of the cuttings to be tended
in the manure by the hen huts,
the day's pruning.

Blue Sage

A bit of sky at the border.
No matter how far into the past
your death recedes, once I think of you, everything
rushes back, as if I'd torn
the sky open, or you had,
lengthening the way to peace.

Clematis

Sometimes a flower is so sexual
I feel the parts of myself
opening, flooding with heat.
I would paint this
the same deep purple
as the flower. Blur the edges
so that the subject is both the flower
and the sweetness of feeling sexual

as I walk through this garden
with my mother, who has mourned you
as you would have wished, her grief quiet
but beyond replacement.

Blue Waterlilies

Reality is a construct, like time.
When he painted these, Monet
came closest to his desire
to paint as the bird sings.
Remember? Only stare at the canvas,
and the water begins singing,
the blue lilies lift their wings.

SECTION THREE

DISSOLVING BORDERS

Long ago in China a poet dreamed of a river
made from notes the birds pour forth
He longed to drink from it
but each time he put out his hands
they turned into a boat let loose on water
or an old bridge laced with lanterns

The poet wept
His cries woke the villagers, though he still slept
What kind of cry is that, ruining
the night they asked
After a while they pressed their hands to their ears

In the morning the poet woke singing of love
as a river that will carry us to death
His song so displeased the emperor
he ordered the poet's exile

That evening the villagers gathered on the bridge
and watched the poet pole downriver
on a boat so small many swore
they were dreaming, though they could feel
the wind at their trousers, the wide planks
the dead had laid with their hands

AND AFTERWARDS, THE LONGING

The odor of raspberry mingling with honeysuckle,
beating through the long heat of a June afternoon
on the veranda, where we lay flushed from playing tag
in the orchard, too lazy to lift the cushions
to the glider or untangle the hammock, chips of gray
paint sticking to our arms and legs, the whole summer
with nothing to do shimmering there before us—

And I'd go back, I'd be that fat flushed girl again
if it weren't that it's taken all these years
to smell raspberries or honeysuckle sweet with sun
and not tremble with longing, not feel my heart
sicken with longing until I have to reach out
to steady myself on whatever wire or rail
the bush spills over, the way I've trembled
and sickened for love, a woman otherwise capable

trembling and sickening for love, for his hands,
for his tongue, the blood-rush, the murmuring—
and the good chair or bed no comfort, the life,
the books, the music, all nothing against this
longing for the beloved to still love, as if love
were all of it, the odors mingling, the blood beating
with what's to come, with knowing there's no stopping it—

And afterwards, the longing—

THE MADNESS OF UNCURTAINED ROOMS

I want to make love to you in a room
so dark you know me by my heat.
So dark you will see me
with your hands. Your tongue.
I want to be throat, nipple, cunt.
I want nothing of our history,
of the tenderness that comes
from too much knowledge.
I want the night to be wild,
and the day that follows
to be wild, I want the moon and the sun
to go on while we stay in the room,
dark cries our only language,
dark hunger all we eat.
Then, when you stand like this at the window
looking out at the lighted bridge,
there will be no need
to understand your sorrow, I will live
dark in your bones.

ALL WE INTENDED

Think of all the harm we intended to avoid, the wild
plum trees lining the walk an echo of this delicate

venture, sustained rain able to topple them like
small monarchs, power tenuous as the faint violet

light Van Gogh pulled across the walls of his room
in Arles, the rest he dreamed, the way I imagine myself

walking past you with the transparency of evening
when I encounter you on the stairway, smiling as if

sorrow weren't the color you were seeing in my eyes,
that moment of silver between twilight and sickness

of heart, oh, you'd know exactly which tube to reach for
if painting were how you told the world what it meant

to walk around with your mind interpreting the play
of light and dark, with your arms about to embrace

being, no doubt about it, you'd have the canvas filled
in no time with truths that bear no mistaking, but

instead you have to settle for the linear progression
of words, one after another, like your own feet passing

over surfaces, carpet, macadam, sand, dirt, the needles
of pines slipping past you like the gleam of skin in rooms

where you've loved while the forest whispers down to you,
a diminishing you couldn't have withstood even ten years
    ago,

only now that atonement offers itself with the quiet of
    wheat
shimmering under the lemon sun Van Gogh learned to paint

by holding so still the blood left his eyes entirely, now
that you realize I never intended things to go this far

past healing or renewal, you reach out for me like the
    branch
about to break into blossom, we know enough, we don't
    move.

HAIRPINS

Whatever you do, don't include hairpins,
an ancient Chinese poet, loosely translated,
advised. Moons will do, or a lone frog in a pond,
but hairpins introduce the mundane
in its least appealing aspect, worse than
a woman who's let herself go or neglected to do
her hair, just tossed the pins and combs
and lacquers aside like a bead curtain
no longer needed to hide the rest
of the room or lure someone into it.

Today, cleaning the downstairs bathroom,
something else the wise would no doubt
leave out of poetry, I spilled an old
cold cream jar filled with hairpins
I hadn't known were there, and I saw
her stride out, her hair streaming
behind her like a Fury's, her mouth composed
against him, so magnificent with wrath
he felt he was watching Blake
etch one of his terrible angels.

The truth excites less: she left without fury,
she left behind things other than hairpins
he's kept undisturbed: perfume, a scarf,
some books. I'd prefer the fury,
leaving as it does less room for love
to continue, but giving hairpins such weight
denies them their rightful place
in poetry, where they should be allowed
to lie hidden in jars, to lie scattered
on floors, to lay claim to the heart.

When I lift it from the glass cylindrical stand
I have to hold it with both hands, afraid
it will slip like water through my fingers,
and even when I pour boiling water down
the smaller cylinder, the infuser, over black
currant leaves, I see how it will weigh
almost nothing, not a teapot at all but the idea
of one, pure as one of Plato's forms, designed
by someone in Germany who must have held still
as handle and spout came clear in the air,
austerely beautiful. That one's in a museum.
Yours is a copy, a wedding gift, one of the few
you got to keep, you tell me, still stunned
that I've broken it, cracked the infuser
as I rinsed the black leaves free.

You're too aggrieved to continue.
Your hands hold the air as if the teapot's
there, and I see her, austerely beautiful,
holding still while you force yourself
to say it, you can't live with her
anymore, her pain enough to shatter
her, and you with her, if it came to that.
As it did. And then her rage, severing
all connection, until there was nothing but
the teapot, its glass so pure you could look
through it free of distortion however
you held it and see back through the pain
to the joys you'd known with her.
I see how your peace depends on her
seeing them too. *If I'd known—*,
I begin, and you look back at me.
There's still time to stop yourself
from saying what will shatter
like glass between us. I hold still.

CLEARING ACANTHUS

The woman who planted this acanthus
loved you too. I cut back years of its slow
spread across the bank above your house
and think of her here, lifting her hair
from her neck to ease the prickly heat
beginning there, beautiful in her
exertion, thinking of you, maybe, of how
you would nod, approving, at this green
precaution against mudslides or less violent
erosions. She's humming. Her children's voices
rise from the deck below, dart around
her, quick small birds. She calls
out to them, shuddering suddenly as shade
from the scrub oaks glazes her skin. In the end,
she rued her choice, you've told me.
Too soon each year the acanthus droops
like the ears of cartoon elephants, a circus
excess its flowered stalks affirm,
rising like tubes of cotton candy,
picked at and abandoned. And nothing
stopped the mudslide when it came.

Last night, you called me her name
again, and I saw what I'd known
all along: how she's everywhere you look,
quiet as light and no less essential
to your sense of this world. And I confess
a grief at that, at not being all
to you, though reason chides me for
such greed and I love you more
for keeping sight of what good
she did you. The ghosts of old
loves are there beside us in the bed,
an article you showed me said: Admit them.
I dig down to see how far one root has gone,

imagining her beside me, her perfume mixing
with my own and the loud sweat of broken
stalks. The soil's clay, rock-stubborn
to my spade. I watch the root disappear
beyond reach, thinking how a name imposes
its claim on the heart: ghostly, dark,
beloved of its own tenacity.

BACK

The doctor's sketching my disks
faster than he talks, comparing them
to tubes of Pillsbury dinner rolls
you whack on a counter till
the tube cracks open,

dough spills out. Three bulging
disks, and fluid spilling out
to press against the nerve
at the base of the spine. See?
These little pouches. He says

pooches, and I feel a sudden tenderness.
How much patience he must have needed
to learn the body all over again
in a second language! A lover's
patience and a lover's nerve.

And all the while I'm thinking this
his blue magic marker makes disk
after disk, flowering, ruffling
at the edges like blue delphinium
until I'm back in Hahn's greenhouse

on a warm July morning, moving
past flats of bright geraniums,
waiting for my friend to finish
her chores so we can go down
behind the icehouse at the pond

and practice dry unyielding kisses
that will do nothing to prepare me for
the first boy's tongue in my mouth,
so quick I'll think of pond frogs,
their tongues licking after gnats.

You've traveled thousands of miles,
the doctor is saying, *your disks*
are like Goodyear tires, if you drive
the car too hard or far they won't last long.
I look up at the small plastic board,

half expecting him to draw blue tires,
but he caps the magic marker,
saying I'll just have to stop running.
I might try swimming, or a bike
with fat tires. Contain the damage

I can't undo. The pain will ease.
He shrugs, kindly, and leaves
to let me dress. I zip my jeans,
pick up my shirt, and feel
my first love move up behind me,

touching the small of my back.
I know what will happen next.
My body will do anything he asks.
My tongue. We learn the language
in a rush, like children.

Except that the charts on the wall
are all English, the office
might be anywhere, I might be anyone.
Ruptured disks are not uncommon,
the doctor had begun. He might have said

We all get old. I stare at the fading streaks,
a while longer . . . blue spires slowly giving way
to the spires of Monet's cathedral, fading
into sky in the high-windowed museum
where you come up behind me, your hands

like heat down my back. In an hour
we'll make love for the first time
in twenty years, in a rush for all we missed . . .
But now, the slower joy of knowing
there's no end to it if we keep going back.

SUNSET WITH QUARREL AND AMPHORA

We're still at the table, sunset,
and he's doing something forgettable,
checking the tv listings, flicking crumbs
from his beard, something that would seem
studied in a painting, which is suddenly
how I see him, stylized, in faded tones
(dusk, now, robbing color), the lines
of his face disappearing
into mask-like stillness while I stare
to fix the moment in my mind—

so that during some other moment
as I'm sitting by the window, the light
will fade, he'll be there before me,

defying time and gravity—his face
mask-like; the background nothing
certain, draped cloth or space,
but nothing untoward, nothing
to make me weep or cry in fear—
he may be as close as the next room
then; long dead; or with another—

long dead, or with another—
how setting them side by side belies
the unequivalent grief they bear,
silently, like women on Greek vases,
thin arms extended to balance their amphorae—
meant to be one woman, endlessly mourned
as she circles the vase?—the vase
itself once bearing aromatic oils
whose scent we imagine
diminishing as we look on—

imagine I'd said *I love you*, turned
the evening back a little, the sky going
violet and rose, the two of us sitting down,
the wine glasses cold, unbeaded—quiet joy
of the still-to-be—not the minor quarrel
neither will remember except as a moment
when love failed—one of the women swaying
with heat or fatigue, the amphora
swaying with her, the oil spilling over,
I can't go on like this unheard.

Why are we surprised by war
when peace comes so hard
between us, when what's said
rarely means what we thought,
when a small thing, a tv
turned too loud, a teapot
clumsily dropped, can bring
rage exceeding reason?

Children stare at darkening sand,
the widow's veil tears the world
apart, the tv screen explodes
the same missile over and over—
In this world, Jean Renoir
says in *The Rules of the Game,*
there is one terrible thing:
Everyone has his reasons.

Climbing the long hill behind your house
after argument, I could find no way
to stop weeping at all I stood
to lose. What reason there,
except that such personal fear
belongs to everyone?

—the soldier clenched in a wind-swept
tent, the general easing his map
to number the dead with pins,
the lovers facing each other
with their empty arms.

Sometimes in the midst of mostly loveless
arguing, you hear yourself trying to woo
like the child you remember only from afar,
voice drifting almost silent over water,
and he, hearing too, catches you up,
saying, *I hate it when you slip*
into that little-girl routine. Stop
trying to hide from the woman you are.

Speak only in imperatives, then.
Order the child out of the room,
upstairs, all the way to the attic
if one exists. Refuse her food,
music, books. Nail thick boards
across the windows, bar the door
from without. Let her pine there
unheeded, voice lost over water.

All this longing for the other
voice, the other face, the other
life. The word itself unfinished: *other.*
Mother. Brother. Another. Seeking
each other while the smell of love bleeds
like lilacs into evening . . . *Usually*
when we win the ones we've wooed,
he muses, *we feel desire go. Like that.*

Opening his hands. The idea of other-
ness bleeding like lilacs into night.
Because lilacs smell of death and desire.
Because, irony guiding nearly all but stars,
he can't grow lilacs in his yard and keeps
sending for ever hardier varieties, guaranteed
to die like all of us. Metaphors everywhere.
—He can't say why he wants lilacs.

Something to do with Michigan, the child
he was then, the sky curving like desire
while he reached for it and the lilacs near,
blooming, heedless of imperatives.
—The greed of the imperative.
Wanting you the way he wants you.
Sweet-limbed lover with perfumed hair
and no more lament than the voice could hold

over one syllable. Love, say.
But you, too, wanting that.
To let your hair fall over him
like water he can catch up in his hands
and need to live. And even then
the endless plenitude of longing.
Nothing, no one, ever enough.
While child and woman weep, unfinished.

THE LIMITS BETWEEN US

I remember everything, the red wood
siding of the cabin, the small door
you had to stoop for, the aspen leaning

with snow, so many deer their legs
blurred together with snow-like quiet
while we stayed in bed losing all sense

of time, taking what we needed, knowing
it was not greed, not anything we had
prepared for, so far had we gone

from the body's limits. I remember
everything opening, my tongue
amazed words could be so unneeded.
But we come back to them, find them
a comfort, because no one keeps that
white heat, you tell me, no one, so

I remember the snow, the deer's dark
legs, the way we didn't even bother
with a fire, the bed so cold at first

I couldn't feel you and then the blur
of being, white heat, yes, everything
offering itself as if for the first time

I keep going back to it, those blurred
hours, and I feel a grief, containable,
that love slows, quiets, holds its own

like a branch under snow, but changing,
I go back and see you stoop through the door
again, the last thing before leaving, see

you walk toward the car, snow spinning out
from your boots, blurring your long legs
while I begin to define the limits between us.

POSSESSION

I call them ghosts, the women
you've loved, though I could call them
on the phone, pass them unknown
on the street some afternoon.
The morning we got separated
in the parade against the war,
I stood still, eyes closed, thinking
something would tell me where
to find you, swim me like a salmon
back where I belonged,
and half expected them
to be there too, instinct
with longing, rage, forgiveness
—whatever moves us to return.
But there you were in front of Chevron,
shaking your head at cops lined up
in front of daffodils, black shadows
shot with light, and no ghosts
anywhere but in my head. You think
I think too much of them, don't
believe me when I say it's not so much
the ghosts who threaten me, though
I often hear their bodies moving past me
in the night like spring-cold streams.
No, the deeper threat's in feeling them
slip through your long thin hands
to me like water, air, some element
we'd both swear we couldn't do without.

FORECAST

Lately I've noticed a preoccupation
with bones. My own, and the bones
of my beloved. Sometimes in embrace
I see us skeletal, and lie amazed
I'm not repelled. For the skull
does terrify, with its holes.
Its canals and hinges.
That this should lie beneath our kisses!

Sometimes we'll be walking in the woods
and I'll watch the cloth of coat
and trousers fall away,
scars and tissue fall away
like snow falling quietly away
from cold branches, and there will be
his bones, his long bones,
smooth and dry . . .

My hair grows long and grey,
I pad along the stream and eagles
see my hair as water, rippling
miles in the sun.
My bony fingers find him,
piece by piece. I build him back.
And my howling, as I rock him in my bony arms,
is a ruinous storm.

All those moments that go by unnoticed, gather into
hours, days, weeks we'll recollect only by exterior

means—the cracked leather autograph book, the diary
with broken lock, the photograph, the photograph, box

after box beside the empty albums, but never the face
we quite recall or follow through our dreams, no, never

complete union between the ones we were and are, so no
wonder I want you in me so deeply I'll feel my skin

opening from the inside out with the sky's slow
rush at dawn, no wonder death made visible in lines

on my face, my neck, my wrists can push the longing
all the way down to the root of me, not the troubled

contradicting heart but that far reach you move toward you,
a coaxing I've never known, your hand, your tongue

moving into me with a sweetness we're told moved into
trees as Orpheus passed, making them yearn after him,

the trembling of leaf and branch, even stones overturning
while the lyre gleamed like flame above them—ecstasy,

the *displacement* of being—this myth we tell to prepare
for the ascendancy of loss, because no matter how sweet

the music, the trees stood still, the stones never moved,
constant play dulled the lyre's frame past gleaming—

everything fleeting, even these words I sing to keep
from turning back, to see the life I have coming

NOT EVEN THEY COULD STOP IT,
AND THEY WERE MYTH

There aren't enough stories to tell
of the moment he turned back.
Some say it made no difference,
the darkness had sunk so deep
in her veins she wouldn't have gone
one step more, already the light
seeped through her skin like a bruise.
Some say she'd long been deafened
by smoke and fire, so his song
meant nothing but fingers stroking the lyre,
and her skin hurt, even that quick touch
was beyond her desire.
Others say she had no desire,
she'd eaten darkness like a lover,
it spilled from her mouth, seeding.
Or she called out to him, knowing
he would turn, it would be over,
because she was tired of being
the one to follow, she had no lyre
or flute, true, but why
should her plain song go unheeded?
But no, he *knew* what would happen.
Beyond enduring.
He could make trees walk
from their roots, stones spin
in the earth, but he could not stop
the dark god's brooding reach
for the days, for the moon
if he wanted it, to ravage her unseen.
So the world filled with lament.
Sometimes as bearable music.
Sometimes not.
Even the animals learned it,
or waited deep in their fur

for its echo: that *No-o-o-o-o*
so endless it makes its own sphere,
travels through space like a star in reverse,
the streak of light like the last glimpse
he had of her hand, or she of his,
drawn back as if in emphasis
of the nothing that would last.

SLIDES

Lightning in the East Bay, the sky
mapped into fleeting states white hot

at their borders while we sit
with the lights out watching

slides from Robin's trip to Costa Rica,
the wall temporarily bare,

the Huichol Indian yarn painting
that usually hangs there propped

against a kitchen cabinet below
the stacked-up papers with their news

of the bird god, Itzam-Ye, the magic giver,
thrust skyward from a Mayan pyramid

long hidden by a Guatemalan rain forest.
Close-up of a fern, its thin fronds

asymmetrically opposed, frail as
the green backbone of a fish

Chagall might have painted in blue air
to remind us of the godhead everywhere

we look. Now a parrot's head, lime
green, the feathers at the throat

packed in like scales. I think
I see the eye move the way glass

beads will seem to move in light,
casting doubt on all you seem to know

about the world. But here's stability,
the thick trunk of a tree spanning

the whole picture frame, its bark
peeled off in strips like brittled

skin or paint. Robin took this one
to count the colors one tree can contain.

Grey, green, silver, rust, white.
Not birchwhite, but the whiteness of a room

no longer there to move through.
Or is it just the nailheads

tapped into the trunk's slow bulk
that move me back to the long room

in the unfinished house where I grew up,
its only walls the outer ones,

no walls within to interrupt the space
I dreamed would change to the material

of rugs, stairs, curtains; the ordinary life
I watched recede each night my father

sat there, smoking in the dark.
The wall flares red, flame-red hibiscus

splashed on branches sleek and black
with rain, natural altar where some woman

stood before the bird god, weaving
red hibiscus through her hair like flame,

dreaming how her lover's hands would cup
each bloom and lay it like an offering

on her dark scented skin, gleaming
by night or rain, how their sighs

would arc around them, incandescent,
the world what world there was

in the long room of their love, its borders
shifting as they shifted, as we shift

in our chairs, the wall a blank of light
now, nothing but rain at the window,

great sheets of rain like wings, fleeting
visions of all we were or are.

Crawl into the corner
of the sorrow you've just told
and listen for the wind to bring you
others: your father's fury at the door
your mother locked against him
when he drank, the night you woke
with someone's hands around your neck
and whimpered *Please don't kill me*
while he raped you raped you raped you, the war
that might have killed your unnamed brothers
had they lived beyond the womb.
There's no end to them
once you begin: it has to do with humans
and with mirrors:
how sorrows multiply upon reflection.
Meanwhile the dog beside you, dreaming
his dog dream, will wake
and paw the door to be let out.
You'll stand there in the doorway,
yawning, noticing the plants
could use some water,
muttering the way your mother or your
mother's mother used to.
Then Spot or Shep or Cloud
will bound back up the steps
and rush inside
and rush about the house like something wild
finding wild joy in every corner.

AFTERWORD

I'd rather let the poems speak for themselves, and speak here of those who have been influential in their writing. Most important is my mother, who taught me to love words before I could speak them by singing to me from Mother Goose, from songs and hymns, from stories she made up as she went along, she now confesses. I don't remember this, of course. I do remember staying home from school in the first grade so that she would read to me. I wish I could report that I asked for poetry, Greek myths, but the truth is I wanted "Cinderella," over and over. Against her own taste, my mother indulged me. She knew what mattered.

The house on Duncan Avenue, where I spent most of my childhood, mattered in a different way. It was unfinished. Picture a huge, flat-roofed, two-storied shed, with a dirt floor, a stairway open as a ladder. There were no interior walls. The insulation stapled to the outer walls was still exposed, tufts of it rotting out or pulled loose by mice. We had no hot water, except what we boiled on a hotplate, and we stood in an old washing-machine tub to bathe. Unless we stood next to it, the oilstove's heat was inadequate. In winter my mother would climb the stepladder on the upper floor, sit near the ceiling. "I'm in Florida," she'd call down to my sister and me when we came home from school.

There were no rooms to escape to, but there were books. Both my parents were great readers. My father was a troubled man, an artist who had stopped painting so that he could work to support us. He drank, often too much. But he had a rich, original mind and a hunger to know things. He read the dictionary like a novel. He loved words and loved to talk; he made us see that ideas mattered more than things. We were sent to private school: Better to finish minds than houses.

I had many fine teachers along the way, but there are two whom I owe an unpayable debt. I took a seminar with Donald Hall during my senior year at the University of Michigan. Hall's great gift to me was to make me understand that poetry was work. Work I could love, work I could give my life to, work I could do, but work. If I wanted to be any good, I would have to stop relying on inspired moments. I can't begin to trace the depth of his influence, or that of Philip Booth, with whom I studied at Syracuse University. He taught me that each word matters, as do the spaces between words. His kindness and clarity helped me be less impatient. I wanted my first book in my hands. He made me see that poems take their own time.

Then, for a long time, more than two decades, I finished hardly any poems at all. I did keep working, though, and when the poems came back, they came quickly. All but one of the poems collected here were written after I moved to California in 1990. But they started with my mother, singing.

for Bob, Cornelia, and Buzz

JEAN HOLLANDER

Moondog

JEAN HOLLANDER was born in Vienna, Austria, and grew up in
New York. She now lives on a semi-wild game preserve. She
teaches poetry writing at the Princeton YWCA and at other
institutions. She has taught literature at Princeton University,
Brooklyn College, Columbia University (where she did her
graduate work), and Trenton State College, where she is director of
writers' conferences. Her first book of poems, *Crushed into Honey*,
won the Eileen W. Barnes Award in 1986 and was published by
Saturday Press.

CONTENTS

MOONDOG

It is not gravity that pulls us down.
Think of the men who stood
on the edge of the moon, left
their floating footfall on the silver sand.
They went home to women, blonde or brunette,
split-level houses, barbecues and dogs.

Tonight the moon is floating
in a tide of buttermilk
fading from tree to tree.
Soon it will shine
a neighbor's uphill field.

I want you to see me
writing poetry in the dark.
A true start but now my pen
awaits your coming, fraudulent
as when I kept our three-month-old
turning pages of her cardboard picture book
to show how smart she was. We sat
and turned and turned until
you opened the door. Now she is gone
should I have deprived
you of that joy?

From the dark trees a low
throb—owl or prey?
The moon's glyph darkens.
She is the goddess of the hunt
and of the hearth and birth.
We are all in contradiction.
The night, on edge of itself
promised nothing.

You are the train whistle of night.
By flashlight I record
your visitation. One shrill
for love, two if you wish
to be erased.

How many cars will pass
before your wheels
center the driveway
curving into home? Now
now you enter. Crickets sing
your praise. It is dawn.
It is midnight.
There is a moon.

PET SHOP

Sunday morning, the carpet of love
unrolls the road to Damascus, takes you
where you don't want to go
and you so stricken with the weave,
the intricate jungle foliage, the tigers
with languishing eyes like does

you run your hands over the cut
texture, read the flowers
blooming for your delectation,
sea urchins suspended
in the bell of your fingers,
the smell of hyacinths washing over
dog food and insecticides

hear the cage where lovebirds sing
a choir of baby colors,
their claws curled all in a row

and you know you have taken
a wrong turn somehow,
moths are fluttering about
and through flickering threads
you can just make out:
Budapest, Budapest

watches his hands
as though they might slide
separate into a B movie
fingers scuttling the rug like a spider
upstairs to throttle the victim

I see your hands trapped in a tight
wedge between door and mirror,
the hotel room caught between day
and night, hands so familiar,
did they really ever cup
other breasts, other secrets?
now white by half-light, fringed
in nicotine yellow, digits clutch
a pen taking memos in another language,
receiver to ear, detached

hands grow hairy in an eyeblink
deformed like wolves' pawprints
three-pointed in snow's crust,
or griffin in ancient showdown
of claw and blood warmth
while at earth's end, somewhere,
a ship is sinking, lapses into sludge
and a sorcerer's sneeze
stirs petrels to circle
as your forefinger dials

a gloved hand touches Adam:
Buddha's index and thumb
form the circle of wisdom.

Ulysses and Francesca, new coupling,
she, her knees raised, spread
at the bottom of the boat, a rowboat,
and Ulysses, hairy, horny,
out of time and seas,
rides the waves of Italy,
the Po gliding between ochre walls,
tops her, his wily tongue
sluicing her ear with smooth salesmanship,
at her lobes like the flickering
flames on his tomb, his scar
riding the undulations of her belly.
He leaps ashore afterwards,
struts his story to old men and girls,
makes Francesca a laughing stock,
but she gets even later
when the girls get together, tells
how he pursued her, in vain of course,
and how she left him miserable
in a bar in Siena, made him
go back to Penelope,
and the girls and Francesca
her story and the swallows
are jumbled and titter
on the wind-swept piazza,
ruffle and flurry, swoop
to the crevices they came from.

This morning I almost played
chicken with a train,
far light nibbling the track
and I was there with three kids who walked
straight heartbeat at it
and the winner a mess
of blood and bones

nervous warning whistles
chase each other
into tunnels of trees, wind, roar
boxcar after boxcar after boxcar
trucks on useless wheels
a whirlwind blasting
blowing me away
on a windless morning
sucking the air after it
and no caboose to announce
the sudden closure—
trees layered in mist

its remembered force like the fury
of ovens in those America-the-powerful
movies in Friday assembly
giant shadows against flaming uproar
smelting fires charged to men's shovels
when geography books boasted
of rails linking America:
apples from Washington
and bloody beef from Chicago
Georgia peaches and berries
and oranges with navels
or without them like Eve and Adam
sunjuice to snowland,
ah we had blizzards in those days
and sleds on the main road in Brooklyn,

while Europe starved we remade the world
in our image, frigidaires and dungarees,
smoke billowing to cloudless blue,
and Humphrey Bogart lit tough cigarettes
from Paris to Morocco,
and all we wanted
was to live till we died.

LESSON #1

I chased veracity
down culverts of meaning,
touched its soft grey pelt,
furless, radiant ears.
A tongue lisped my mouth.
Its white belly lied.
Later I saw scratches
on my arms and legs.

The birds are truthful,
calling to each other
over and over
but my ears intercept
no meaning.

THE WIND WITH BEAKS

Watch yourself,
see how you slouch
to the feeder every morning:
bird's eye view from the cardinal's
staccato cry, bright head of woodpecker
bobbing just out of sight

deliver them
from having to comb
the wind with beaks,
fill the station
of their hungry granaries,
entice them from flight

here windows are their only danger,
unforgiving margins of air
and to me
the wrinkling seasons:
wheat and sunflower seeds
day in, day out.

STOP

do not look at the moon

it will make you want
things you cannot have

do not look at the leaves'
bone/gold shiver in the night

or find fox fire cushioned
on the wings of an owl

let lamplight keep you warm
in its yellow cocoon

let it keep you warm

THE MANDARIN

is redolent in the garden,
his hair entangles
frailties of moss and aphids
his armpits fester wilted leaves

he cannot live
another night below frost line

only the loquat blooms in October
a dream of bees hovering blossoms
their syrup fragrance at his nostrils,
petals cluster his flesh as he sleeps

he is homeless

he has left his cover of embroidered satin
at the last guesthouse, given over
his last cumshaw gold piece

he shall never recover

he will be crushed
in the seasonal struggle of hemispheres
in this indecent meeting of spring with autumn:

loquats in blossom
and snow to fall

the stench of rickshaw sweat
breaks his heart, and the noisy
clatter of shoes on stone jangles

his memory. He knows it was not better
when that land was forest,
decades of pine needles soft
under bare feet. There were arrows
and blood, the long night booming
to temples of sorrow,
venom served in curved cups
cold from the fangs of nightshade:
dread of unknown gods smoked from the altar,
when life was swift

now his days scuff slowly
and death waits, numb at the gate

he watches
red leaves of sycamore
fall to rain

he feels
a cold snout nuzzle
his bones

two-thirds of his life. Bent
to the ratchet of time he studies
the ground for stones, distrusting
the flat earth. He stumbles
when shadows take form.
He has forgotten
the routine of labor
trapped in mid-stamp approval
while the wax hardens.
His clerks note his indiscretions:
an inkwell cracked, a dribbled garment.

He remembers the smell of pasture
on a day he was thirty
having come from the city to the mountains,
cows grazing below him,
sunset wind abundant
with fragrance of cud.
He still feels the porcelain cool
of flower-rimmed childhood baths,
weight of his father's hand on his shoulder
first time he scratched the complex
character for man.

Now moments of wisdom show him
how quickly wormwood encloses
a sudden radiance.
Bite of ginger in dumplings,
or rim of sesame oil on his soup bowl
warm his yellow hours.
He sleeps through long afternoons.
In his dreams he whimpers
cries of the squirrel caught by a marten.
He hears his own heart at midnight.

SLOUGHING

We leave remnants of flesh behind us
where we've lived

last year a dog
buried in summer grasstime,
easy dig

hamsters in stiff cages,
cats under wheels

drips of monthly bleeding and winter fat

a lover's semen leaking
after parting

always time sucks
flesh from tender places

until aged, we float weightless
above thin rooftops

THE CONCLUDING CRY

"Aoi" ends the dying song of Roland
on the battlefield; his gauntlet hand upraised
cannot sustain the struggle, nor his lungs

the sound. Now banished from the air, aoi
is the wolf cry of abandonment

the dry scream dredged from the black holes
of mouths in a Munch painting

aoi is the strain to howl
that cannot raise a moan
from the dream sleeper

it is the real scream that surprised
my mouth in labor

it is the headlight glare
of deer draped over cars
of pigs hanging from hooks

it is the photographed stare
of Somalian children looking out
when the film runs silent

THE CHOSEN

I try to tell them how it feels
to be chosen for death

how a child accepts
the policeman no longer friend,
that men, in and out of uniform
are looking for you—

how you've been prepared:
"Jud!" "Jude!" "Judin!"
with snowballs that didn't respect
even your parents. Streets were not safe,
gangs waiting at the last corner
each way home from school

how terror softens you
and laws anoint
you for your bitter fate

how having been
in the jaws of that beast and spat out
does not make you kind,
how you bite back at the innocent
instead of the brute offender

how it has taken you a lifetime to shut
the pages of that bestiary,
to stop fearing
footsteps on the stairs

how you cannot find
a reason to have been spared.

AFTER GOING WEST

Three sprigs of lavender
my son brought back for me
after hiking with friends,
and I no longer invited

the manhood I raised having come,
the stubble awkward on his chin,
he reads Hesse and Salinger
and not the books I thrust on him

I think his frame too big
to have come out of my womb,
I renounce the baby head pushing, I give
the freedom he has taken gladly

crawled out of comfort,
he has erupted mothering
and I am happy, tired of the labor,
and touching his separate skin

for the second time I feel
the wonder of that parting.

ON THE ST. PERPETUA TRAIL

"We frequently lost our way in this compacted meat . . ."
from The History of the World in 10 1/2 Chapters
—*Julian Barnes*

We often lost our way
arches of devil wood barring
our every turn . . . ferns covered
welts in the earth . . . we stumbled
avoided swamps
leaves big as shields
ferns clutching our legs
sweet fragrance of meat-eating darlingtonia
their cobra heads nodding
emerald in wet wind—
butterflies and bees clambered
down their deep tracheas
followed the sticky nectar
down to digesting tracts

grass snakes slithered the path—
a coral snake with red/black/yellow markings
threatened, raising its venomed head

we followed trickles flowing to rivers
curling white over spiky stones—
tadpoles flickered in rock pools,
leaves and ephemerids swirled
to where the ocean breaks,
Bob's Creek flowing to salt
in its pebbled channel
down to the crush of waves
jelly fish pearling the tideline
dead cormorants washed in with leavings
of crabs and broken clams

and in all this, how
shall I keep my son from danger?
I want to put up signs all over
skull and crossbones in ordinary places:
that kissing bugs are really assassins
eating each other and leaving
painful bites in our flesh . . .
that deer crossings do not warn of automobiles,
nor rock zones keep stones from dropping,
that cars take the right of way
when he bicycles on the narrow
line between wall and cliff,
that scrambling up rocks, his lost footing
will not grow him wings,
that after a friend's diving
from the roof into drunk-dark water
his skull did not crack but for an inch

where shall I find words to tell him
meat around bones is fragile
flayed like his favorite T-shirt
the neckband holding peeled fabric
to his chest . . . that even his flesh
against water, metal, rock is compacted
to slush quicker than coupling made him
that what holds him into being is thin
and translucent skin

STRINGS OF MOURNING

for Elizabeth

Hands cannot hold
nor could Aeneas embrace
the shade of his father, arms stretched
around space and finger-ends touching.
Still, nothing goes to waste
flaked fur and feathers gathered
into nests again, blast of wind rooting
seeds in a better place
ground warm under last year's hay,
air great with geese rising from the lake
in spring's phantom restitution.

Remembering Job's children were not given back
new sons and three fair daughters took their place
I give away
the dress she never wore
to be filled by another.

A child in Vienna, I saw a painter decorate
our kitchen wall, watched as his patterns shaped
green brush into green grapes
berries out of red paint
plums purpled into frames—
but know no colors to inlay
her white-washed space
not other children, nor the way
of forgetting.

Like seaweed under waves
heart flows to love or grief
and the pain
is greater and more bearable
than you imagine.

GRIEF

Her ghost lingered about the house
when we came back after burial,
the evening full of shadows and the night
black with fists of pain. At dawn
the meaningless sunset rose again,
light returning to the empty crib,
birds calling with freed beaks
and our heater chirping against autumn.
Food regained its flavor, the stew
we had heated, but could not eat the night before
not too dry yet. A few more days' sunlight
dappled the windows with moving leaves,
petunias climbed the glass with sticky tendrils.

We were consoled, though her death
still flickered in our dreams,
giving her back and taking her away
in glimmers under lids.
We were free to hear other news,
laugh in the open and move
to sex in the dark.

Now years have almost cleaned
our house of grief,
until she suddenly appears
fleshed as she would have lived
in bright colors.

ELIZABETH, UNDER SNOW

As I walk to your grave
across fields under frail sheeting
of spring snow, more precious for being
brief, even as you dwindle in your coffin,
I raise you to long-legged beauty,
the sounds you made as a baby
turned grown-up, we hold conversation.
The dog who never knew you rambles
leaving clay pawprints, four-pointed circles
on thin liming of white.

How you would have loved this morning:
bare dogwood tossing in wind,
forsythia in yellow-starred brightness,
clusters of glistening crocus,
snow melting in their corollas like teardrops
and arrows of wild geese striking
quick clouds in a dark blue sky.

A turkey vulture soars down, flies over,
black Aztec-cross markings
as sharp on its white-winged chest
as the pang of twenty-year sorrow
fixed in my breast.

THE LOCUST TREE

I hear the news: latest statistics prove
Babies should be put to sleep
On their backs. Knowing that

Let me turn her about.
Let me get up at her cry.
Let it not be fated.
Let all of them come back
The whole bloodied fantasy brood.
Let the other child, a girl too
Curly haired and dark like me
And the boy, blond blue-eyed
Miracle that later was
Let them come to breakfast
German shepherd of my childhood dreams
Gathered at their feet
His paws touching the lion-claw
Legs of the table. Let the boy
Throw bits of cereal down at him
The girl giggling claps
As I slap his hands, gently
Just enough to pink his skin
Warm under my after-kiss.
Let them eat and grow flesh
As my real children did.
Let them rise from their dots of blood
Their wattles and pigeon bones,
Their spaces filled
With sail-swell of new wind.

After so many tears
Is it morbid to think
Milky pajamas of her sleep
Diaper I never changed
I guess the mortician did
But not pin her up again

To think what remains:
I who loved her all
Could I love what there is?
A reproof of worms
Coffin cracked and gone
Nothing of hers when they dig?

Petrified, she lives.

They say locust wood keeps
Until the day after
A stone melts.

A KWAKIUTL WOMAN SPEAKS
TO HER DEAD CHILD

> *". . . a mother hauls her dead child in her arms, weeping over it.*
> *She has had carvers and doll-makers make all kinds of playthings,*
> *and they are spread about. The women wail, and the mother speaks*
> *to her child. . . "*
>
> *from* Patterns of Culture

Why have you done this to me?
As soon as you are strong, come back,
I wait for you, my breasts are aching
to give milk again, this time
no painful passage waits for you.
You chose me once, waters of love
poured from me at your birth.
Why did you go away?
In one night you took
my offerings into the dark.
Did you think they were toys
carved by paid strangers?
What I gave was flesh
carved from my bones,
my blood your color
and your life the life I almost lost.
Love made me forget the pain
of your head shoving into breath,
your need to be—so strong
they could not hold you back.

Do not be angry, come
from the deep place you've gone.
I will not test your breath with feathers.
I will wipe the gravel from your lips,
wrap your cold skin with wool,
warm you with brightness of my wish,
get strong, come back to me.
This time I'll spread my legs
to give you birth with the same joy

I open up to take you in,
only do this for me, move in my arms.

SUNDAY, 6:15 P.M.

"Hold fast till I come . . ." Revelation 2:25

Trains collide.
Through speeding windows they unfold
in flickering frames: a student going back
to study for exams, the salesman practicing
his pitch, a couple dozing on each other,
a young man, taste of lover on his lips,
safe behind drab shatter-proof glass,
the freight train bunching black
at a siding, the surrounding air   .
not yet sucked into brakes.

Let us stop them from melting into puddles,
ice them like the ship
frozen on a sea of glass, the men savoring
their slow dissolution, holding fast
to the cold that numbs them into warmth,
six-winged angels hailing them
with golden candlesticks, their flames
melting wax to stalagmite snow columns,
blankets and cots riding the star-crossed air,
their contortions stretched, glorified
luminous at the crystal horizon.

THE CALLING OF PETER AND ANDREW

Christ floats,
his feet not touching stone,
as flat-eyed fish glow green
in transparent water.
Peter and Andrew raise
a net of air and light.

There is no matter,
only spirit taking on
the act of color.

But when that moment broke,
and Peter crucified, head down,
exploded in red paint,
did he remember Christ
floating in light to him
across suspended waves?

The mother thanks the man
who rescued her son
over and over on different screens
and you can see she wants to hug
kiss him as though he were the boy
fallen down the sixty-foot well,
his spine broken, and this common
scrawny man lowered himself
down into the funnel
of the underworld, an Orpheus
without song, coupling
his body to the fallen flesh,
brought him up into the bright
glare of surgery where they saved
the boy again, and pinned to microphones
the rescuer says: "I went down
and got him out," as though he would
do it again, if need, tomorrow.

NUTMEG

The scene is nutmeg autumn,
grizzled with rain and clouds.
Each in its white and black
pattern the cows are spread
across a trampled field.
Winds tug at ochred leaves.

Our hands still on the wheel
or walking from the mailbox to the house,
between saddle and stirrup suddenly

swifts flutter white with underlight, sky
opening to let the first sun in,
flames up the top of a yellow beech

and this hangdog world
is clear and bright
and we want to live forever.

PRUNING

Getting ready for indoor winter
I pull up spike weeds, cat's ear,
clover, and shepherd's purse,
intruders among jasmine and orange trees,
groping tender greens with coarse fingers
to trim a brown geranium shoot
that sprouted hidden leaves.

"I'm doing it for your own good,"
I told my children before poking
a splinter under skin with a needle,
a speck under the lid, a slap
for lipsticking new-painted walls,
avoiding their fear-bright eyes.

Now I stuff the broken stalk
back into soil, telling myself
"It will root."

PERIWINKLES

One day we brought
the periwinkle from the woods.

My shovel cradled clots of blooms.
The kids in boots: the boy
clutching a pail of roots and mud
with mittened fingers, his sister
at his side trying to fit
the worms that dangled from the rim
back in their earthen grooves.

Now every winter on this trampled patch
behind the house, teal leaves of periwinkle
green whatever snow there is,
and every spring before the daffodils,
the ground is studded with
five-pointed stars of amethyst.

Tonight the trap almost worked
but failed at the last moment.
My husband wants me to help

set up the two swords,
six prongs and heavy spring
that won't retract.

I do not want to kill
blind moles, those hunted
underground selves of ours.

I refuse to help. He's furious
at the coil he cannot pull
at the mole that got away

at his uneven lawn, at the brown
snake that squatted in the sun
but would not eat the shadow mole.

He's furious at me
will leave me
with this mole-dug lawn.

He thrusts a pitchfork
at the earthen run—
triumphs in bloodied prongs.

The night
is smeared with moonlight
luminous with owls.

COW POEM

This is a poem to celebrate cows,
how they cluster under trees, black
where I turn in at Amwell Road
or grey-brown on the foggy slope
of Conover's farm, trampling banks,
rivulets, ponds, sharing meadows
with wild geese.

I celebrate the cow flying
mid-day over Kandersteg, then higher
over the alps to the butcher's,
rope halter to the helicopter,
legs dangling in repose. "Is she dead?"
No, only the living don't stiffen,
bend so gracefully to swoop
of terror, noise and wind.

In the 16th-century chapel, Bach
bellows against narrow enclosures
of white-painted stones. The organ
unruly, large and imprisoned
like the rat nested in my oven
dashing against frames of fire
to my feet when the door opened—
sound hurtles from wall to wall.

I celebrate 23 cows in America
killed by one stroke of lightning
"Good way to go," you said—
no blood-smelling death truck,
no yank-up throat-slit panic.
They had gathered in fragrant pastures
and were gone, like Old Testament prophets,
their meat still good.

This is about the cows in Switzerland
who are not afraid of lightning
or thunder, but go on grazing,
shredding sharp grass and thistles
in rhythmic snorts—
clusters of flies and dung
washed in the shiny downpour,
they move to the clangor
of fragrant bells.

And about the old farmer, long beard,
shirtless, his ribs skeletal,
scything the steep grass field,
resembled the grim reaper,
too dignified for picture-taking,
working all day against storm clouds,
stopped only to sharpen
the sickled blade.

This is to celebrate all cows:

those browsing on the path to Fulpmes
standing, sitting, not moving,
barring the narrow way

a red car overturned
off the new-rain glossy highway
ambulance gone and a cow
cropping the grass

and elsewhere, after the rain
and the wedding, the cow
on her way to high pasture,
prodded with sticks and honking,
fallen on the slickened pavement.

"Cows are smelly and stupid," you said.

DUNWALKE

Mare Imbrium
the Sea of Showers on the moon.
The cows are real enough
bellowing across tracts of grass,
real as the cars' uphill exhaust—
the sky hysterical with clouds.

"Baby, the rain must fall . . ."
Your tongue plagued my ear.
After we kissed your mouth was dank,
Sea Scrolls from an unopened cave.

When I awoke to a scream
was it in the street or in my throat?
A white dog barks at the gate.
We have pressed the mute button.
His jaws open and close.

Flies awakened at six,
scrubbing their eyes with tufted feet,
buzzing each other in frivolous longing.
We hid under sheets,
found lust in the Song of Songs.

Now deer run from our walk, waving
the underside white of their tails.
This and their startled snorts
mark them prey—it is their nature.

The buzzard tree is full.
Osage oranges litter the road
warty rinds broken
inedible yellow
exposed.

After she left him they shared
the same sky, seasons, stars, full
or thin-sickled moon. Some nights
she could see him, picturing her
picturing him into infinity
like the logo on Dutch Boy paint.
The way it was between them
no one understood, wires entangled,
enmeshed by lightning.
Nerve ends fagged out, she faxed
her longing to his. On the phone
always a woman's voice
though she called at all hours,
and he unwilling to get out of the grave,
those cemeteries in Queens
where Manhattan ends, and the dead go.

She wanted to be a witch
to call him up out of the Bible,
she wanted to believe
in hell to be with him—
of such strange things her conversion
as the medallion on her breast
testified, as if confession could make
things happen. She confessed to nothing
except she wanted him
to share her grave.

GROOVES

Rain, coming down on snow today
is the same, is not the same
flakes swirling last week
and love was the same
is not the same
ten years ago
or yesterday:
brightness marbled
to a dry cough.

No one will be seated
while the play expires.
A woman sings "My guy" into an ad
salting my open heart.

Time
to turn the radio off.

She is an old woman, hair dyed black,
has come for a new life in America.
She cleans houses, finds dirt
the other woman left.
She rushes to finish but falls behind
in a whirlwind of dust,
tabernacles of mousenests
wads of cotton and eruptions
of powdered foam rubber
under cushions and rugs.
Consort of Lime-Away
she is the enemy of scruff,
working against this house—
its stain and tarnish.

Is this what she came for?
Victor translates her chores:
the house to be done in three hours.
She has sweated five and still
not finished. Is this better
than a commissar, better than
a drunken husband?

She wears her hair in bangs.
When she gets home
she will take a scented bath,
she will dress up in high heels,
she will dance.

The woman in the velvet hat—
two purple roses quaver from the brim—
is shaken with palsies of regret.
"I took the Amtrak," she says as if that
would excuse her being,
while you trudged through knee-high snow
slushing in at every step for this,
her tongue slithering timetables and scraps,
and you confused, trying to read them
upside down, sideways in the mirror
of the compact she thrusts
at your rain-hooded head
now wound to her song like a cobra,
turning your snakeskin inside out.
She is gone with the next whistle,
the trestles bending to take her in.
She has left her lip-smear
in the air. Your cheeks are numb
with the kisses of mourners,
your way back a snare
of black ice on tar,
and far away your house
is neon with Christmas lights.

Real green was sparse that spring,
the grass down-trodden and the trees
bristled with unleafed wood.
We stayed with friends at your insistence.
Our windows gave upon a park
named for azaleas, but the air
was scarred with rain and nervous pigeons.
Imprisoned in that room
I watched a careful mother place
paper on which her child should sit
to play in the sand. I escaped
to the museum.

           That night on our tight bed
I saw again the women with soft Rubens flesh,
and from the pose of the madonna peeked
a peasant girl holding out one milky breast
through the slit bodice of her blouse,
the embroidery on her blue cloak
needled in painter's feathery strokes

and falling into sleep I was
the Flemish profile of a young betrothed,
her breath caught in the strict
vest of her jewel-laden dress,
tight pearls on her long neck,
her hazel eyes fixed on the edge
of background glowing emerald.

THE MERCHANT'S WIFE

The Victorian lady,
petticoats blown and billowed
is standing at the seaside,
bodice tight
against her fluttering
unaccustomed breath

She has walked out
to the waves' embroidery,
bits of shell and froth
at the edge,
her parasol a halo
against sun and wind

She is flirting
with the long-legged silhouettes
of two gentlemen

She is not thinking
of her sour husband
thirty-two years older,
or his belly rubbing
on her flesh,
nor the snort that announces
his cessation

She has left
the twelve-year-old slavey
with her lice and stories of monsters,
brushing the Persian carpet
as dust swirls back on itself

She has left
stench of bleach and brown soap
rising from the cellar laundry,
the washerwoman unable to scrub

rust of old blood from
her stitched-rag menstrual pads

The Victorian lady at the seashore
in a strict blue taffeta dress,
twirls her ruffled umbrella
and smiles, a coquette.

XENOTRANSPLANT

The human gene transplanted to a pig
insists on itself
I am, I am
is not rejected
in the brain.
They both grow wiser.

In this confused Eden
we shall walk with God.

The narrow-minded, stubborn salmon
insists on reliving his innocence,
flipping his brightness
against rocks and swirls.

Flickers no more. Dammed, has become
food for small fish. Come look
the whale, the great whale
is a young one, spouting upriver,
meek in sweet water.

Somewhere a mother calls,
the shuttle of her weaving maw wide
with algae and grief.

He spouts, lit by boats and binoculars.
He will die sounding.
An item in the *Astorian*.

Let us go backwards, mix with the orangutan
before he learns to speak: alone, true,
I want. In truth we lie. Let us go back

to origins. Shun lepers,
or their bells will ring
from every steeple.

Let the sea take back
its narrow strands.

Though rocks cluster with mermaids
like ladybugs bred oh, the disgusting
swarming orange and black inlay moving
on a peak in Colorado, hand and foothold
teeming with half-winged bugs

We are not Ulysses, will not mind
mermaids singing, adjust
our headphones and jog.

The government will rescue
hurricane houses, declare an emergency.
Save us from ourselves.

The doctor will unzip his bag.
Santa Claus with syringes. Save us.
The baboon will be one with the giraffe.

The fat sow will be prevented from squashing
her newborn piglets with human faces.
Wedge her in a box. Put her in the stocks.
See. We save. We do good. We made her too fat.
Never mind. Let her stand up and suckle.

Let her stand up. The sea swells with syringes,
with blood. Let's hold hands and hold it back.
Let's hold hands and circle the equator.

Let us clutch. Claw of bear and nail of tiger,
monkey's digit and skin of newborn,
clenched claw to back. Round the circle,
hoot and holler, we are, we are.

Quiet.
Listen.
Wingbeat.
Agitated feathers.

Hands cannot lift
the would-be fledgling
nor can beaks assist
flight or fall.

Each dawn
one bird wakes before the others.

The sun rises on all.

Let us begin with pride
of lions. Their amber eyes disdain
the sloth of bears
dreaming of honey
and shoals of silvered salmon.

We have hung
the bear bag too high.
His anger unpitches our tent,
lines loose in crumbled soil,
frail fabric shaken
by fierce gusts
of his tremendous appetite.

My sleep tugged upright
by his shadow bulk, or is it
soft skulk of foxes?
The brown eyes of dam and cub
are wise. They have judged me
harmless as they stood,
penumbras in new-risen light.

Let's go home to shelter,
windows screened, doors painted black,
lights bright against the stars.

Twice I have heard nightingales
sing on their watch:
twilit oracle at Delphi
and from moonlit silhouettes
of pines in Italy.

They will soon be hung
in doorways of butcher shops,
their legs tied in clusters.
They will be eaten,

bones unfeathered after mass,
crunchy Sunday snacks.
A charm of finches, spring of teal,
a murmuration of starlings.
I have glimpsed
coveys of turkeys in our woods.
A shadowed green, indistinct they are
unbelievably ugly and beautiful

as are does in herds, or solitary
giving birth to a dappled fawn,
the buck always alone
in agony of hunt like St. Eustache,
and elks in their gangs pursued
by a kennel of dogs in full cry.
They race to the front
of the tapestry. In the back
I have stitched the howling
of a mangy bitch in Sicily,
her ecstasy of pain, a Gehenna
on the way up to the view.
Two thieves in the parking lot.

Better to think how gaggling geese
rise from the water each spring,
necks and wings stretched
into skein of flight, taut,
they unwind between the poles
without arithmetic. For us
this is the sixteenth spring.
Next year, the plague begins.

"Just because you were born in a barn
doesn't mean you're a horse,"
said the man born in Sweden
and became a Latvian.

Vienna bore me, but my heart is wrapped
in the American flag
like a soldier's coffin.

Does a tree yearn for its roots?
Our Christmas tree didn't know them gone,
stayed green until Easter. Cuba undid me
with its Latin tongue.

My father, the sacrificed Isaac,
never recovered, neither did Abraham
(Sarah made sure of that)
God's voice deflected, bent
to a rustle in the bushes,
a ram rendered for his beloved son,
servants left below in the ordinary
unthinking way, witnessed only
what was allowed. And Christ,
cursed with cut-throats,
accused by every corpse that swells
or does not swell against nature,
saved only one. High-wire (look,
are those wings?) walker,
died rather quickly in the usual
afternoon sandstorm darkness,
no words to describe the glory.

Nothing. Words clamor and fail, must
like the joy of vultures,
witness of worlds from a windspan,
descend to their hunchbacked

baffled forms. Entrails reduced
to neat jottings on parchment.

Judges, kings, strangers,
homeland here and everywhere,
one faith among a skyful
of alien gods. Caravans winding
past deserts, mountains, a continent,
the promised land, a rented mansion
occupied, milk and honey rippling
across owned groves. Every man,
woman, infant and animal
put to the sword. And weary,
after stench of slaughter, start over.

In its pit the untested snake
knows its venom, the skunk
his odor, the hawk, his plunge.

We test our knifeblades
against our tongues. Sons
of Hagar and Sarah at war again.

Still, the hora circles
its Latvian-Arab song.
Cossack killers on horses
and their long-ago victims
ringed in one Tartar dance.

Tongues tangle: Old German,
Hebrew, Slavic. Desert
and blue-eyed barbarian
merged—a new animal
born in the barn.

FIDDLEHEAD GREENS

He told me I'd never amount
to fiddlehead greens, or so I heard
having just eaten a bowl of them
all curled up tight at dinner.
He really said: a hill of beans,
though I don't see how that applies
any better, when Mom showed him
my A composition about a man in Spain
who denied his belief for years
finally yelled out he was a Jew
even if it cost his life.
My uncle said I must have copied it
and Mom folded the pages away.
She served some trickly sweet dessert,
while we sat around the table
at the top of the slanty-floored kitchen.
Years later uncle pronounced
my engagement ring false,
the stone too big to be real.
I know the diamond was real enough,
but everyone said he could tell.

We stopped at edges, games,
small facts and tokens,
told sexy truths from the Old Testament:
Bathsheba, David,
Susanna and the Elders lurking,
Lot's salty daughters
hot in some cave
until he drunk and wifeless
two nights got his their way.

Those lucky girls
to have a father and to have him too
while here we chatter, you
grown old and feeble, keep
nursing home hours
until I cannot see
how I once loved, desired
you, gnarled and rotten—
until renewed on screen

King Kong in hirsute grandeur
magnificent ape machine:
impossible suitor
impassioned destroyer,
appears and I surrender, cower,
cling to the only lover
animal—father
fur suit caressing arousing
whispers of ancient dreams.

RESIN LEACHING FROM OPEN ROOTS

This wedge
slit from the trunk
when the uncertain saw
crosscut the redwood tree
on the descent from Maiden's Peak
here leans against the window,
a thin slice of seasons
or a waning moon
more like an Indian
his beak-nose squashed
against the window sill,
his angry knot-hole eye is fixed
on me alone, his scored cheek ruddy,
wrinkled striations on his brow
(or are they warpaint streaks?)
his hair of hennaed bark
crimped into the formal braid of chiefs.
It is the face of my father
vexed at this restraint,
eye that saw everything,
high forehead and high cheeks
down to thin lips—
I don't recall his kiss—
Sundays we played
his hand the doll I cuddled
baby I consoled
until he stopped the game.
I see his wooden profile on stiff sheets
his heart and brain wired to a machine,
his mind already elsewhere.
My tears drip
the hand he moves away
when I let go.
Today I weep

the child your hand foretold,
and you, father, frozen
in the crystalline lens of an eye.

TABLES

after Czeslaw Milosz's Table I *and* Table II

Table III

Polished to a gloss, this table of heavy wood
Is taken up, shines in excluding candle light.
Three figures hover, backs to us, at the buffet—
Newly arrived friends? waiters? customers?
I cannot tell, as in a family photograph
I puzzle unfamiliar faces for relationships,
Hair and eyes monochromed to shades of grey,
Nose and brow, a slant of chin, mine, or an accident
Of parallels, interlopers, not even friends, shapes
Who fit into the framed event, as we do here
Drawn to this food, these candles cut into the dark,
These stars now stirring in the velvet negative.

Table IV

The stars now stirring in sky's negative
For us, have not yet risen for the ship that bent
Its passage past our stretch of ocean into deeper seas.
There the sun is setting as it sank for us an hour ago,
And will again dissolve into the coral waves.
Their present, our past, will resubmerge at future rims.
The boat that bobbed the water at the end of our dock
Briefly outsailed the sun, as we in passion think we do
Until conniving night thrusts in. Silhouettes at the buffet
Will turn, reveal themselves; the stars contort
Into astrology. This meat, this bread, these pewter cups
secure for us the gloss of ancient wood.

WHEN THE STRINGS OF MORNING OPENED

I

Beginning of vacation, the old house waiting
to repossess us, time not yet wound
to clock's turning, at breakfast
pattern of green-gold clover still noted
on plate and cup, taste
of just-plucked grapefruit
tart/sharp and sweet with morning
night still clustered in dark
groves now in fruit and blossom
seasons suspended as in Eden
before time was

II

when the strings of morning opened
mocking birds awoke us
with light-winged variations
of clucks and cantankerous flutings—
windows open, after the tight
winter house we had come from—
air new and fragrant
with flowers of orange and lemon
limequat and grapefruit
and named for a French navigator
Bougainvillea rooted near no ocean

III

drying its wings in dawnlight
a monarch butterfly flattens
against the window screen—
inside, through thin wire tracings
I feel its goldenrod glimmer
the fuzz on its thorax, dazzled
as a bluejay plunges to beak it
sees me, reverses, flutters
to black-tipped wing upswing

IV
next day on the slope of San Gorgonio
hot snow in the sun around us
and smell of pines
manzanita, ponderosa
yews and flaming blue sky

I think of weathervanes swirling
away from the wind that moves them
as yearning turns from its fulcrum
of time, to the past or future
in a hurricane of craving
except for this now still moment
this center, this eye

V
veined by such fragrance
feeling has gone to flesh
and flesh is porous, unweighted
body floating in light as exotic
fish in aquariums uncurl
their feathered fins unfurling
cobalt, coral and aqua
as before they moved in deep oceans
their gills absorbing exuding
at one with the gravitous depth

so I inhale this morning
swim in the open fresh of the day—
old attachments
daughter and her first lover in Oregon
flowers and rain at the windows
son in the Smoky Mountains
his trees in the mist beginning
their clamorous leafing
and last night's lover/husband
are swirled into my motion

are now, are here
throb in my blood stream
San Gorgonio snow melting
sluicing down Persian fountains
river-runs inside me
as now in moist places
desert anemones bloom

                    La Quinta, Spring 1989

AFTERWORD

Although I teach the writing of poetry, much to my surprise, with apparent success, I have no pretensions to theories of art for my own work. I do know that a poem is not a piece of furniture. It cannot be sat on, eaten, worn, or even used for comfort. Although poems may at times console, they may also make us feel worse. If I write out of some despair, the act of writing sometimes turns the knife deeper because grief sharpens it.

When I begin a poem I usually do not know where it will end up. If I foreknow the result, why bother? I do not know the techniques or tricks of the trade I shall use until after I have done so, when the poem proclaims itself finished, or unfinished, as the case may be, to be put away, reworked, only perhaps to be declared unfinished again. I try to wrest my thought or feeling into light. It is an act immediate and ugly, a brutal delivery, sometimes a stillbirth, always a struggle. There is no time for theories or pondering the way. I keep hoping that each new poem will be different from, and better than, the last. As Joyce Carol Oates said some years ago: "We write out of a sense of failure." After the completion of each work, a writer feels that he has not said what he had hoped to say and therefore must, like Sisyphus, roll that stone uphill one more time, and then, once more, after each try, in that glorious hell of creation.

I do know what I admire in other contemporary poets and therefore try to teach: the stark image, the beauty of simple, everyday language—verbs made powerful, unembellished nouns that earn you the right to a rare adjective, words honed to a sparseness almost harsh, and striking metaphors that once introduced, ring true.

Poetry can never say anything new, and therefore is never out of style. A poem can only let us see and understand truths we already know. I think a good poem reaches the heart and mind not as an abstraction, but as a hammerhead of fact, a reality. The famous toad in Marianne Moore's imaginary garden is more memorable and real than the toad who hopped, thoughtful and slow, across our terrace this morning. Every time we reread a good poem it seems new and unique, and at the same time obvious and natural. These are my "rules" of poetry. I do not know if I obey them. I hope I occasionally do.

DAVID CITINO

The Weight
of the Heart

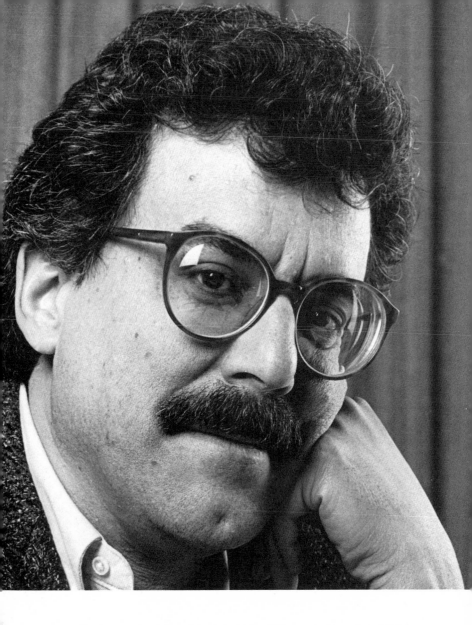

DAVID CITINO is Professor of English and Creative Writing at Ohio State University. Among his honors are poetry fellowships from the National Endowment for the Arts, the Ohioana Library Association, the Ohio Arts Council, and the Alumni and the College of Humanities Faculty Awards from Ohio State University. Citino is the author of seven books of poetry, including *The Discipline: New and Selected Poems, 1980-1992.*

CONTENTS

I. LABOR DAY

To make Grandfather's shack
I cross sixteen pairs of track,
oily ties, snow-bright gravel beds.
All around, B&O diesels thrum tunes
that tickle me, teeth and tongue.

I climb the stairs and wrestle
the door open to the insult and glow
of the gnarled Italian cigar,
his fat smile and that
of the squat, pot-bellied stove.

Now I'm walking with Father
through the GM stamping plant.
What is this—the din of hell?
He helps me cover my ears
but even so, at seven I'm made

to know in each small bone
there's much in a life
a laborer must leave unsaid,
and some work hurts a body
just too much for words.

Some Saturdays he takes me
to the chemical plant,
and while he does his paperwork
in the dirty office stall
one of his friends speeds me

squealing in a growling towmotor
down glaring warehouse rows
long as cathedral aisles,
spinning me and tons of feldspar
on wood pallets in and out

of boxcars bound for mysteries
like Canada and Tennessee, where,
I imagine, other boys stand
at the loading docks bathed
in sweat, aching the taut joy

of knotted muscle, shirtless
in the fierce, fatal strength
by which they make and spend
their lives, ready
for an honest day's work.

THE BETRAYAL OF THE FATHER

In the years before
he became angry,
he loved the company,

would relate to us
proudly at table
how the president's son

or some other big deal,
pausing in parking lot
or zipping up in men's room,

had used his first name,
asked "And how about
the wife and kids?"

handshake and smile
saying they two alone
shared a great fate.

It was a matter of trust,
of love tendered
and returned. Later,

after efficiency experts
had watched for weeks
with their stone eyes,

and the promotions
went to those who had
youth and college,

his face changed,
work began to hurt
not like a bad tooth

or ache in groin or gut
but like a fist
squeezing his heart hard.

His father had gone
from peasanthood,
a supple-spined *Contadino*

in black, earth under
his nails, to Laborer
and then Foreman,

walking fifty-three years
of B&O ties, the railroad
a benevolent father.

Father grew bitter, nights,
over what someone with
a great suit and hair style,

Italian shoes that shone
like pools of oil,
hadn't said to him,

eyes that wouldn't,
no matter how he'd try
to fix them, meet his own.

MY FATHER SHAVES WITH OCCAM'S RAZOR

Entities must not be unnecessarily multiplied.
—William of Occam

The simplest of answers
is preferred. Explanations
of the unknown should first
be sought in what is near.

So with love and poetry:
what we can't make out
we seek in the seen,
ice, fire, stone, steam.

Shaving away another day
I recall watching my father—
flecks, specks of soap.
Ooo, blood! Such longing.

Where has he gone? Not
cloudward, to rise and fall
on wires taut as harp string—
and what parent ever

was consigned to fire
ever and ever?—but here,
a rectangle on the wall,
every morning mirror,

darkness between lips,
a song, this very voice,
the blinding light of eyes.
Each night he grows in me,

appears at dawn at the end
of dream, his hand moving
in billows of steam.
And just like him I bleed.

THE QUANTUM MECHANICS
OF FATHERS AND SONS

Taking the measure of one photon
changes the nature of another
from the same source, both
hastening toward opposite ends
of a growing, shriveling universe.
Just so, the oncologists's scalpel
in a pink Florida clinic
entering my father's flesh
draws bright blood from me
the same moment in cold-rain Ohio.
The X-rays Father was dosed with
to burn away adolescent blemishes
scar and pit my own skin before
he tells me the story. I'm pale
still from waxing, waning moons
we viewed, our faces glowing
in Cleveland starlight,
the backyard nights he'd catch
in his hands for me, fluttering
like fireflies, sparks of eternity
flung off a God who, the promise was,
always was, always will be, always
will remain the same as the God
of Moses, Curie, Einstein yet
who needed a mother and son
and a night full of stars
to feel complete. What drops
into the surgeon's tray,
life gone crazy in atomic clocks
of the cell, I'm lighter by,
precise estimates of memory,
shifting constants of parent and child.

BREAD

Companion, from Latin,
one we share bread with.
To the tribal child
I played at table,

it was no unfamiliar,
but un amico di casa,
a family friend,
or even God Almighty,

who could mutate
to the thinnest wafer
light as the word light
on my dumb tongue

yet sticking to the roof
of the mouth as if
to postpone the inevitable,
digestion and elimination.

Slices of life, a way
to tell time, grandmother
stooped, Sienese braids
powdered with flour.

Still today, in this age
beyond belief, days of pap
wrapped in plastic,
we expect of it so much.

How I'd choose to go,
if it can't be toiling
in sweat among vines
of purple wine and love?

Taking a gold loaf
from the oven, its scent
spinning the room
back to childhood dreams,

cutting the rough crust,
easing the blade
into sweet yielding meat.
For this is my body.

BREAD FOR THE DEAD

All Souls, *Festa dei Morti,*
we'd go to Calvary or Holy Cross
to bring them back, saying
their names, calculating age

by two stony dates,
the death and resurrection
of darkness. The rite
of the family, to remember.

In old times food was left
on mound or stone,
small sweets, bread
shaped like boat or soul,

new bread and lentils
set out on the kitchen table,
the windows ajar so
the hungry ones could enter.

So thin they'd grown,
I'd imagine late at night
in my bed, listening
for the ghost-guests below,

clinking silverware
and chewing so slowly,
talking softly so as not
to disturb the sleepers.

Grandmother at the funeral home
theatrically throwing
her small body
on the corpse, kneading

the soft, pale face.
O Pop you look so nice
all dressed up—
but where are you going?

We children weren't sure.
Maybe like us, after having
to endure all this,
he'd finally get to speak

and eat, sit at table
with the family old, dressed
in their best, breathing
the scents of fresh bread.

It's love, the erotic of morning,
bell-loud, I'm made to think,
this fight to inhale light again.

Having recapitulated phylogeny,
I don my heavy humanity, the suit
of bone and suet. What's this I hear?

They name themselves: Dove Rueful,
Robin Trill, Maestro Song Sparrow,
Gruff Chuckling Grackle, Exploding Crow.

Trees too sing names to every wind,
Soughing Oak, Rustling Hickory,
Whisper of Willow, Hissing Ash.

My alarm: the dark silence had gone on
too long. Moments ago I lay still
among stone, deep family graves,

but every waking, for a moment
I'm every child. I remember praying
for the kindred dead, myself,

"If I should die before I wake,
please take me to heaven,"
a place where trees could speak

and children fly like birds
beyond a rainbow. I begged favors
for those near me, but prayer

was fear of fire, malevolence
in God's unblinking blue eyes.
He'd want to hurt me—and not

in tripping playground ways.
Could I stand against omnipotence,
outfly my brimstone Frankenstein?

I knew something in hell beneath
or heaven above Cleveland I'd be
allergic to, coughing and wheezing—

tree pollen, mold, spore—my asthma
so hot she'd kiss me on the mouth
forever and ever without amen.

Still, for all the bliss and terror
of matinees, I began to doubt
the awful boredoms of eternity,

a place with no tolling dawn
or fear of night, no sexual din
of breathing, birds and trees.

SENIOR CLASS PLAY: *A MAN FOR ALL SEASONS*

I pull on the gold tights. How wrong
this feels, the family jewels exposed
to 32 rows. Every teenage sense screams
loud enough to *jar my liver loose*
from its moorings—Mother's phrase
when, alone in my room but just for her,
I crank up Dylan:
For the times they are a-changin'.

I'm backstage on a folding chair,
St. Ignatius H.S. stenciled on back,
rhinestone-sheathed dagger pricking me
underneath. My hat's grand plume
trembles when the blower kicks on.
This play will make you think,
the director, suave in soutane,
Roman collar and beret, had warned us
through rehearsal. *You don't*
examine your lives, my good men,
you're no better than dogs.

I wear pancake, lipstick, rouge, but
mine is a middle-linebacker Henry VIII.
I'm furious with Thomas More
and *the full-fed hypocritical Princes*
of the Church. I'll brook
no opposition, Thomas.

How good it tastes, this bombast.
First true happiness I've known since
Kennedy was blown apart
the year before.

On the plane back to Washington,
Johnson, hang-dog usurper,

CITINO 19

hunkered beside the widow veiled
in grief's chilly thrall,
the world fading like a prom flower.

Enter stage right—flanked by
sophomore retainers rigid
with their first rush of politics.
I've been on the river, I say,
looking down at my well-turned leg
and, with amazement announce
to the house, *Look, mud!*

Laughter down the aisles
swaggers and swells me. I turn
to glower across the stage
at good Sir Thomas More. Later,
at the curtain call, after
too many words not my own,
the death of a man the world held
such hope for, I know the dangers,
mortal and intoxicating,
of even a little power.

Ancient strata below us, tiers
of our lives. In this heap of steel
built over bones of Erie warriors,
I think of Grandfather, a name so hard
that from Ellis Island to his wake,
each time someone tried he'd be born again.

Do names erode like flesh and stone?

Not far away, beneath grass green
as the outfield, he's resting from tales
I made him sing and steep climbs
into the cheap seats in this stadium,
to watch the Indians sweep
out of the dugout, the organ bellowing
like Easter. After, he'd wait hours
so I could get autographs,
Doby, Rosen, Colavito, Vic Power.

Now I myself am history, beside a son
who finds solace for bourgeois anxiety,
a society of the unconnected,
in this wild Celtic keen and drone—
a son who once, in Dublin, too American
in Levi's and Reeboks, camped out
on the mean south bank of the Liffey
outside the band's recording studio,
hoping for a glimpse of real heroes.

What do we get from history but a list
of names, a few melodies? "If
it's not one damn thing, it's another,"
as Grandfather put it.
Now our prayers are amplified
to state-of-the-art thunder
that aches deep in bone.

In the name of love, One more
in the name of love, words
youth won't let die. *No war! No war!*
When my son shouts it's my voice, my fist.

Three times Grandfather was drafted
by Emperor Franz Josef. The fourth time
he ran until he'd discovered America,
invented the mandolin and my first song.

He called me *Honey-boy* till I turned sixteen.

On stage, as we knew he would, the singer
picks up a spotlight, flashes it
on the crowd. The whole world
a dance and chant, we're caught,
father and son, past and future
unspeakable beyond this moment of light.

Near forty, devout
as The Little Flower,
she's taking her medicine again
so she won't have to think
of her four children,

hiding with their father
and his girlfriend towns away.
The day her mind began jangling
like a pay phone
on some urban corner

the teachers pinned her down
until the cops ran in
to drag her to the cruiser
in front of her children
and two hundred others.

Tommy's mommy's crazy as hell.
She became the spectacle
her mother always said
Catholic kids should never be,
screams like bald tires

on a misty mountain curve.
Each night she kneels in her bedroom
at the Board and Care
saying the rosary with the man
who made her pregnant.

She reads my poems to him
and suddenly angels
leggy as Vegas showgirls
fly from the pages
and light on the television,

a demon with Sinatra's voice,
Reagan's aw-shucks chuckle,
mustache like Wayne Newton's,
croons to her. She tells me,
Snakes are coming from your book.

Her pain strikes the satellite
and falls back. I say,
A man who'd take advantage
like that? Pick yourself up
by the bootstraps. Leave him.

No. He's all I've got left
except for the lithium.
Time for medicine. Eyes closed,
she's wearing patent leather shoes,
anklets, a dress bright

as a new soul, as candles
in a winter cathedral dark
as her mind. She opens
her mouth. Something moves
inside her as beautiful as God.

DEAR ROBERT: I DREAMED YOU WERE DEAD OF AIDS AND NOW YOU ARE

I watched the undernourished undertaker,
fingers stiff in his ice-box lab,
try to shut your eyes. Over and over
they flapped open, window shades,
one of those cartoon moments the kids
we were together years ago would love.

Finally they stayed. You looked asleep,
but later, at the funeral home, I knew
that alive you could never lie still
through that canned Jesus music.
The mirror I held to your lips returned you
unclouded. The only pulse was mine.

There was weeping, you'll be happy to hear.
A few even looked inconsolable.
One woman caressed your face.
It was lovely watching her touch you
but you and I are old enough to know
it's the rarest love that resurrects.

Her high heels beat a fading tattoo,
perfect thighs whispering *Goodbye.*
(I swear I didn't try to follow.)
As first dirt tumbled on you I awoke.
It was my alarm. My God, I was relieved.
You must believe me. My grandmother,

wise Calabrian, knew that evil dreams
mean nothing but good. It's the vision
of fine friends, happiness and cash
that tempts God to cook your goose.
I've always admired you, but never
that much. At times it even came

to something like love, didn't it?
Remember college in Athens, the knock
on my 3 a.m. door, your abject plea,
"Prove to me that I exist," and how
I slammed the door on your foot,
opened it and said "There, damn it,"

making you laugh? Are we guilty
of what transpires in the terrible dark
that frames our days? If I had my way
we'd all live forever. My grandmother
would be here today to vouch for all
I've said, and you.
                        Sincerely,
                        David

THREE VERSIONS CULMINATING
IN THE MINIMAL

1.

Every poem's the news: you're dying
of something incurable. In this case,
let's say a chronic degenerative disease
of the central nervous system,
the myelin sheathing your nerves

flaking away daily, no matter what
you do or don't, an entire wildfield
of chicory and Queen Anne's lace
scorched by Malathion or Agent Orange,
spasm and jerk, a lack of balance,

so damn dizzy, a thriving, pretty city
charred dark as timbers of an urban house
the arsonist kissed, spine sizzling
wild as butter in an untended skillet,
high-tension lines before the twister.

2.

Every poem's the news: you're dying
of some incurable disease
of the central nervous system, field
scorched by Malathion, Agent Orange,
char of arsonist, high-tension lines.

3.

every poem's the news you're dying

Serrastretta, in the stony Mezzogiorno.
As my sons and I send three twisting streams
into the dark and ancient public loo, I know holiness.
Age, basil and lemon are an unction on lips, fingertips—
the way love can stay hours, a lifetime.
Above these three seas of Magna Graecia we inhale
so many last breaths, bloom and doom-perfumes,
musky ruins, rocks of ages. "Give me a place to stand,"
Archimedes boasted, "and I will move the earth."
It did move for him, great tinker of Syracuse
whose magic gadgets held off the triremes of Rome—
catapults lobbing rocks to crash through hulls,
grappling hooks yanking dreadnoughts out of the sea—
still it wasn't Ares he revered but Aphrodite:
he wasn't alone in that bath. What propelled him naked
into avenues of history shouting *Eureka* was not science—
water's displacement, densities of silver and gold—
but the tides of wishing for a buoyancy beyond
our mortal gravity, thrusts and moans of love
pure and simple. Now I'm told that we Americans,
tossed out of Spain, want a base for F-14's
in Crotona, the Crotone where Pythagoras lived
with the students he loved, women and men,
as equals. He taught them what I've tried
and failed to show my own children, not to want
this world too well, to demand of the self a reckoning
before sleep: *Which duties have I neglected?*
What harm have I done? Wanting the air pure,
they ate neither flesh nor beans, loved
all past lives. Love of wisdom was their adoration.
They wouldn't harm a louse or grub,
yet when the Master found
that the square of the hypotenuse

of a right triangle equals the sum
of the square of the other sides, he was
so overwhelmed by the universal beauty
he sacrificed a hecatomb of bawling, shitting oxen,
even though he believed in nothing
but the struggle of one self toward
the arduous good of all, this southern Italy
a place both sacred and holy where
the body can grow so still
a soul could stand close to the sea
and hear no plumed roaring or thunder
shaking death down from the sky,
only the grand whirling ditties of planets,
a dance of stars and the oceanic human heart.
We three zip up and step outside
into the nearly perfect light.

THEFTS FROM ITALIAN CHURCHES
REACH ALL-TIME HIGH

—Difficult economic times to blame

The teeth and jaw
of St. Anthony, patron saint
of lost objects, stolen
from under his nose,

the Franciscans in Padua
had to offer up
The Prayer of Intercession,
Si Quaeris Miracula,

"If you're looking
for a miracle," to ask
the saint, what's left of him,
to try to find himself.

St. Lucy's body
was romantically poled
down Venetian backwaters,
a rippling throw-rug of moonlight.

The miraculous blood
of Sts. Gervase and Protase
was sucked, siphoned from
Perugia's cathedral.

Nothing new. The Venetians
kidnapped Mark from
Alexandrian darkness
to gild their tourist church,

and Bari fishermen
sailed home low in the water
with a Christmas catch,
the corpse of St. Nicholas.

An altar boy, I was warned
to lock the church behind me,
to keep God and gold plate
safe in the tabernacle,

art on the walls, as
the neighborhood rotted
around me. The streets
are mean even to angels.

Hard times for the sacred.
We give for precious rag,
old stone and bone
all the market will bear.

Art leads us to temptation,
lust for more than
our ungilded, mortal days,
economics of beauty and truth.

No matter how I trill, flail
the tongue, how strenuous
my fingers go, it won't come.

In this preposterous terminal
where fascists meant to amplify
each word to state shouting,

I'm deaf and dumb. My Italian,
an unholy glossolalia which
started out Calabrian anyway

and thus already alien in Milan,
sounds even to me stiff as
the dead and elementary Latin

I muttered to high altars
of my youth. We're drawing a crowd.
The agent, sweating with abandon,

tries to tell me yet again
how to reach *bella* Cosenza.
He's insisting, eyes bulging,

that the Rapido train, once
it gets to Paola, will strike
a mountain, ending all trains?

Someone will come to fly me
over the peak? Then I hear *autobus*,
the same on several tongues.

Sí sí sí sí. So hard it was
to be touched by this stranger
and his eloquent gibberish

that I've been made to see
it's communication that's always
the problem, our echoing ache.

A lifetime it can take to mean
and get what we think
we need to say safe across

the great abyss to any other,
and every victory means
irrevocable loss, just that moment

what we thought, what we felt
and frantically ransacked
our meager baggage for—

and finding it at last,
the very word—gone, unless
the sleek highspeed train turns

to rock, screeching to junk
on the grade it couldn't make,
and swooping suddenly earthward

out of mountain mists in time
to fill us with the divine joy
of knowing the language,

the miracle of the bus.

On a bed in the Hotel Cicerone,
just off the Piazza Cavour, weary
of the dark marble of public life,
we turn our thoughts to America.

Trash of emperor and tourist,
divine lovers with stony genitals
drove us back to afternoon love,
maids tiptoeing past our door,

tittering like sparrows. Now,
swaddled in sheets, your leg draped
on mine, we watch *Name that Tune*
in Italian, the Roman bus driver

coming up with "Be Bop-a-Lula"
in just three notes. Who are we,
beyond franchises, cheap songs?
Transients, drifting countryless.

The old Romans said *patria*,
still the Italian word, *fatherland*.
Our parents rent their earth
beneath neat New World lawns,

headstones crooning surnames
in the music of the mother-tongue,
folk tunes and steaming manures
of the peasanthood we can't elude.

Who can flee two dates, a name?
Yesterday another American couple,
Rolexed, moussed and jeweled,
called a proud old waiter

"a little chattering monkey"
because they couldn't comprehend
his attempts to please. Glasses
of Frescati shook with his shame.

But when we said each other's name
I swear I heard singing with us
that city some call eternal—
though erosion tells us different—

human love like a prayer, *O, O,*
a wild delight loud enough
to flutter and blush the maids.
An emigration, this has been,

but in reverse. We've come
this far to find our parents gone.
They've left us a lust for music,
so we sing of their place

days beyond today, a country
where each breath is fierce
as steerage, and where, they say,
the streets are paved with gold.

II. The Sorrow of What Flies

WHILE CROONING "LOVE ME TENDER," GHOST OF ELVIS MAKES LOVE TO ME: NOW I CARRY HIS BABY

Take away the night, and what are we
after all? Sides, joints, hocks
of spoiling meat. Photos exposed perfectly,
wens, pores, warts and all. Battered
again and again by the beery, sweating weight
who calls me wife, I'd grown
suicidal, horny for deepest hell,
until the night of the worst beating,
as I lay alone, every part of me
bruised, and that voice began
with the wind moaning down the chimney,
that form not yet running to fat
from drugs and Hostess and little girls
in white cotton panties,
the leather jacket tough and supple
as a birch trunk in a storm.
He moved me, there's no other way I can
put it to you. It took us
only twenty minutes to create the world.
Next morning, when my husband
rolled over cruelly to have
his will with me, responding
to the habitual stiffness
the way any beast seeks to slake hunger,
he found nothing but the shape
it took my body twenty-one years to make
in the mattress. Now the me he has
is the damnedest lie, the one
I've become free as dream.
There's a music we can make of memory
scored by wildest, dearest wish,
the joy which comes from opening to
the hard throbbing body of God.

PHIL OCHS IS DEAD

You've given me a number
And taken off my name
To get around this campus
Why, you almost need a plane . . .

The fatal miscalculation after all,
duding you up in pompadour
and monkey suit of gold lame
to try to manufacture
some charisma, and break
a *protest singer* into the Top Forty.

One fat bratwurst in that sad get-up,
you couldn't understand why
the masses wouldn't throw off
their chains and dance to your art.
Three chords a song—
for this was folk music—

the bosses cracked the lash
on backs stooping for United Fruit,
Marines with good teeth
hit the beach at Santo Domingo,
young men, limbs whole, jaws
clenched, left for Vietnam.

Call it peace or call it treason,
Call it love or call it reason,
But I ain't a-marchin' anymore.
The proles you praised for ignobility,
time-clock humpers bulldozed
like landfill trash into company graves.

Too many martyrs and too many dead,
Too many lies, too many empty words
were said. No one read you, not even
as a kid-journalist at Ohio State.
"Fifty Phil Ochs fans can't be wrong,"
your own record company cracked.

Yet more than fifty came out
to Carnegie Hall that last time
to hear you stumble, drunk, through
the Conway Twitty tune.
A barrage of pennies hooted you
off stage, but you returned,

belly a fire of uppers and wine.
"I'll try, wearing this gold suit,
to sing a song of significance,"
you shouted above the roar.
And then, "Elvis is Che Guevara,"
which won them over a moment,

but during the Buddy Holly medley
the booing turned bloody.
Few but the truly buzzed stayed
to hear your bogus Elvis:
Well, since my baby left me,
I've found a new place to dwell . . .

at which some smartass shouted
"Where's Phil Ochs?" And then
the chant, "Phil Ochs is dead."
When management pulled the plug,
you begged, "Give us back
the power." It was for you

I played the teenage Red
at the penny-loafer prep school
in Cleveland's Little Puerto Rico.
Nights, I'd lie about my age
and sit in black turtleneck
close to the stage at La Cave

to study you spidering
the frets, the righteous frown
of your inflection. I learned
to flat-pick my fat Gibson
your way, sneer at injustice,
heart bloody with conviction,

and ache for the laborers
who walked stiff and near-deaf
out the plant gates, eyes fixed
on a world of fat empty,
the lost girls and boys who hawked
their perfect bodies.

Wed the word to its humanity,
you told me, and you'd
make a world where cherishing
all others was the only work,
work brought souls to justice,
justice was something to believe.

THOSE OLD SONGS

We've had our arguments,
this irascible old pal and I.
Too much I've put on his shoulders,
heartstrokes taken as my right.

At times he's been the straw man,
barn-loft *whoosh* of combustion;
other times a log vexing the stream,
damn Polonius, a royal pain,

Fat Mr. Oh-Oh, all thumbs. Yet
how once we'd leap and ride.
Now age slithers up to spy.
With a child's eloquent reticence,

worry-lines mapping our path,
he ladles out his heart, mortifying.
Sorry as can be, feigning devotion,
I listen late into the night

to those old songs of the body,
the list of half-imagined wrongs
against our just cause,
the fatal necessities of life.

A tale of our times, of a type too common.
Still it showed me—holding my daughter
on my lap during the radio news
as she read to me—how sorrow can fall
silently as starlight, ooze down
from the attic to stain the kitchen table,
how some words burst over the dam
we erect to keep a life high and dry,
furniture floating about the rooms
as we seek safety in trees, constellations
brimming on the water's surface,
how stories collide with stories, and how,
for all our late dumbness,
language still can work too well.

It goes like this. Martha was heard
by her husband, Ted, working in the yard,
to have screamed at their daughter, Daisy,
"Now you'll get what's coming.
Get into that bathroom." When
he came in some time later he saw
Daisy face down on her bed under a blanket.
He knew her by the feet sticking out, pink
from the water, as pretty, he remembered,
as after evening bath when she'd come to him
all scented and cuddly for goodnights.
Always the feet made him think
of mourning doves rubbing against
one another. He pulled back the blanket.
Her face was purple as a bruise. "What
in hell'd you do?" he demanded. Martha,
four days off her lithium by order
of the doctor who feared her pregnant,
told him the story, as frantic,

able to comprehend almost nothing
but numbers, he tried to dial 911.
It goes like this. Shadow their cat
had become Satan two days before,
whispering vile obscenities from the mouth
of the handsome television anchor,
hissing an acid catechism as he lapped
at his water. He'd carried the rough evil
on his tongue and passed it to Daisy.
Martha read the 666 scrawled
in disappearing ink on the girl's forehead.
She knew she had to wash it off.
"It was not my fault," she said as she told
the story to psychiatrists, attorneys,
prosecutor and judge, and once back
on the medication, she no longer heard
the words she'd described as
"a steel claw gouging out the right side
of my brain." Precisely what *innocent* means
she was. What can we expect of language
beyond its brute occasional truths
woven through silence to make our human sense?

Nestled on my lap, feet tucked beneath her,
my child still pages through her story.

It goes like this. Children, lost
in the woods, hungry as can be, come upon
a house of gingerbread. In the house
an old woman, an oven, a cat. Just as
in real life, things happen, some wonderful,
most horrible. If my daughter heard
any of Daisy's story, she gives no indication.
The lost children live happily ever after.
Shadow, no longer possessed, has lost
the gift of speech. Martha is unable

to feel remorse, but sometimes she weeps
because, she says, she can't weep.
She is back with Ted, who says to her,
just as before, "I love you."
They still believe in words. They plan
another child—a girl they hope.
They will not name her Daisy.

VAGRANT FOUND DEAD NEAR RIVER

Caucasian remains ragged as the landfill,
hard as dumpster refuse were discovered
by a passerby at 6:01 a.m.
alongside tracks rusty with dawn
at West 3rd and Commercial.
The pocket mirror held to rigid lips
by the first patrolman on the scene
stayed clear as plate glass
of BancOhio and AmeriTrust uptown.
Flesh bore the pallor of scrubbed smoke
from Muny Light, eyes frozen open.
An Assistant Information Officer
of the Police Department refused
to release his name until it can be ascertained
whether he'd any relatives, owed anyone money.
He'd been arrested 683 times for vagrancy—
in a land where possession measures
at least nine-tenths of law, a real crime.
No evidence of foul play, but they'll cut
just the same, weigh each organ
on bureaucratic scales. The City Fathers
will do him homage with a pauper's grave.
May all buses of the Regional Transit Authority
and every tug bending ore carriers

around river curves circle his grave,
horns mourning,
the last department stores downtown
fill windows with crepe, city women
doing their business remove their platform heels,
pimps step out of their Lincolns, heads bare,
to follow the cardboard casket,
crack runners remove gold chains, unlace
their British Knights.
O Citizens, let's chant requiems
in the piss-stained cathedral, offer
on the flames of arsonists
two pigeons heavy with lice,
two herring gulls, two pit-bulls,
two Norway rats fat as bursting trash bags.
This fallen urban man, sure as we're born,
will rise again to walk among us.

Proxima Centauri, beyond our days
the nighest shining, needs 4 years
and more to make our dreams.
Andromeda's nebula spends 900,000 years
to teach loveliness to would-be seers.
Our own Sol by now has spun us
15 billion years past the Big Bang,
God exploding into time and space,
suns and colds. Yet some distances
infinitely nearer ache us more.
Wilhelm Roentgen discovered X-rays
by navigating the spaces
between the fine bones of his wife's hand
which the night before had opened to him
in passion, his vision moving us
through everything but nightmare skeleton.
Between any two galaxies or gods
space freezes the mind, any two bones.
We're born to separation.
Nearly all that is we're in sight of
but can't get to from here
except in the homage we're made
to pay each particle of matter
in us and beyond, mysteries of distances,
the love we owe the stars.

THE MEANING OF APRIL

Elemental, this belief in a city evening glossed
by rain,

winds declining like the cries of nighthawks, earth
too intimate.

You inhale, and mud insults the brain, last year's leaf.
Bloom and rot

an exhalation fragrant as mother's breath, familiar
as the dark

beyond the bedroom window of that interruption
in the world

the perfect little beast of light and mud you were
called home.

POSSUM

for Warren G. Harding

The final cemetery mile this morning.
Chasing my breath through
a world softened by sweat and fog,
night's every vestige, I realize
scents of life and death are the same:
damp of old stone, earth
freshly turned, wild onion and mint,
mums fading like a lover's face.
Sun kindles tips of oak and sycamore,
shakes free to scrape down mossy trunks
into crabapple and redbud,
empty eyes of marble-garbed angels
poised sexless between this world
and the only other. Sun
ignites forsythia and history,
sad tomb of Harding, hollow
as a life lived for reporters
on a front porch in Marion, Ohio,
between his speeches tiny cries,
furtive cloakroom fumbling
with buttons, corset, hose.
Now light catches the possum full
in its white skull face,
stopping him between trees,
freezing me too six feet away.
Neither has anything to fear
yet neither of us moves,
sun carrying on its genesis-labor,
squirrels scrambling down shagbark,
sapsuckers rattling their elms
accompanied by gruff cackling
of great-tailed grackle and jay.
Finally, this bad dream twice the size
of a Cleveland rat scurries

from me and all the light of day.
My destination must be the other way.
For all the ache deep in thighs,
I can still pretend I'm a child of dawn,
young enough to accept the promise
of another day, all that's written,
even those figures formed of stone.

OCTOPUS

Arms awave in semaphore,
blushes, dots, bars

traveling its surface,
its own syntax and grammar.

The poem of itself,
flesh become thought.

No split between mind
and not, language and blood.

Both symbol and object,
the very thought of it,

hunger, fear, satiety
revealed in posture, pigment.

There can be no failure
to communicate, no

privacy, no hiding
from the brute truth

of folding and unfolding
but in these clouds of ink.

If a tree falls in the farest forest,
no soul near enough to hear, what
have we lost? If, while we lie
rapt in sleep or human love,
millions of songbirds pass
above our beds, who will keep time?
Our parents knew dolphin cry and humpback,
heart's bubble and suck, primal tides
grating over stones to make melodies
old as anything. They whorled new words
from mouths of conch and cave,
measures deep and unceasing. Later,
clinging to their trees, too deep a sleep
meant a whistling fall to earth,
bloody thrash, hiss and fang
of terrible lizard. Night
was the sacred fear keeping them alive
to the keen and hum of every star.
Today, if we stay awake to all
that flies, we can hear the perfect cries
half a mile high, the singers
riding time's crescendo and diminuendo,
vireo, warbler, wild canary, thrush,
song sparrow, purple finch,
beating wings toward trees of home.
Such art sets the bones to trembling,
hammer, anvil and stirrup, even
the soul vibrating like tongues
of larks. Eternal voices, wings
bound for the same light
wings of parents sought,
the sweet killing wind breathing
through us all night long.

So heavy can be life lived in air:
a moth, *Lobocraspis griseifusa*, drinks only
the tears of elephants, while

hummingbirds, to keep tiny hearts rattling,
must find their way each day
to the secrets of a thousand flowers.

Pecking years of carrion-eyes, shells
warm and baby-blue, lunar fields of roadkill,
a crow can grow so callous it must

roll around in a furious hill of ants,
lashed by formic acid, fiery heart-bath
just to learn to feel again.

August twilight, skies grow holy.
A nighthawk climbs the ladder of air, dives
all the way to miracle, scream of stop

inches from earth, a song, lithe rise
of cut wing, heart pounding in throat.
Flight is always fatal, in time. The bat

hangs seven years of its ten in a torpor
atop rising stalagmites of *guano*, but awake
can pick a gnat out of ebony heavens

in a rollicking breeze, a shadow haunting
the planets and stars, hunting its own screams.
It's no wonder, then, for all the light

playing about them, that angels
are said to mourn in organ moan and throb
the brutal truth that no matter how hard

they go at it, beating indifferent air
in blind white flurry, they can't touch
one another, wings light as morning mists

off the river of their unrelieved perfection.

III. The Cholesterol Levels of the Gods

SISTER MARY APPASSIONATA ON
THE NATURE OF THE HERO

Arthur whips sword from stone;
Rama takes up the great bow.
Mary squishes the snake's head
with her pretty, immaculate heel;
Madame Curie just glows.

Odysseus pokes his fear
in its one eye; Columbus,
for all his glistering greed,
lashes himself to the mast
to weather gales of doubt.

Bright as Hermes, Roadrunner
dusts Coyote at light speed.
Nolan Ryan ices a magic arm,
climbs the mound to hurl
heat at the Angel of Age.

Isis, offering her breast
to baby Horus, becomes
Madonna with pudgy Bambino;
Pharaoh ascends his throne,
the lap of the goddess of death.

Daniel nails the old lechers
who came on to Susanna, while
the Manhattan prosecutor,
that Giuliani guy, asks
just the right questions to slam

the cell door on pinky-ringed,
hard-on neighborhood boys.
My heroes! You're something,
you know, laddering
up Sinai, K2 and Matterhorn

or strolling moony seas,
centuries of mortal contention
with lion, swan and bull,
but even more, you're
the daunting dare hurled

at some mangy private demon,
the taut-lipped *I'll change
this life,* the stilling
of a clamorous self, pure merge
of temporal wish and will

into a shining timeless deed.

SISTER MARY APPASSIONATA PRAISES
THE SENSE OF SMELL

> *Houses and rooms are full of perfumes . . .*
> —Whitman

Lion and lamb, lion's den
and sheep pen, ardor of Adam
and Eve's sweet cunning fruit—
only nothing smells the same.
To safely make it through
this blooming, awful world
we must sniff out the difference.

Teachers live longer, inhaling,
every period, youth's essence,
lessons licorice-sweet,
salt of dew on downy lip,
chalk dust erasing wrinkles,
chafe of damp corduroy,
ringing change of the hour.

Socrates knew a new bride
needs no perfume but innocence.
And not just beauty speaks.
Power too breathes out
its name: while his armies
blackened earth, Great Alexander
stank of blood and violets;

after noon, the left armpit
of a certain nobleman of Paris
exuded a priceless musk—
you can look it up. Sorrow
takes away all sense of smell,
anger offends like the flare
of sulfurous lucifer match.

History's a dog-eared tome, sheaves
of mildew. Scratch and sniff:
St. Therese showering roses on us
from above; that stench which says
Sin Here; baby's sweet, sour kiss,
the insult of ammoniac age,
our bouquet of every day.

Since 1830, the Pope's signed off on
only seven appearances of Mary.
She fancies Western Europe:
Portugal's Fatima; France, at
Lourdes, the Rue de Bac in Paris,
La Salette, Pontmain;
Belgium's Beauraing and Banneux.

At Fatima, the year Lenin whacked
the Tsar, breathless Mary announced
that the 1917 Red machine
would mean a heap of trouble
but then go up in smoke, fumes
of a vodka coup, unrumbling tanks
in 1991. It's all come true.

The local bishop makes the call,
whether Mary has dropped in
for real or no. She hasn't been,
skeptics say, to Lubbock, where
rosaries riot every Crayola hue;
nor to Bayside, where her X-ray eyes
expose the Pope as a Rich Little fake;

not to Medjugorje, where the bishop,
his land loud with tribal death,
wants to check the I.D. of someone
billed as "The Queen of Peace";
and not to Youngstown, where
the sun pulses like a fat old heart
although the mills are cold.

She visits only the holy lonely,
teenage girls already aroused
by other miracles—bitter and bright

as blood—and dying to believe
a mother can remain intact,
assume her heaven without
going the loose grave way.

It's no accident that The Institute
for Marian Research sits near
Wright-Patterson A.F.B. in Dayton,
where sleep those frozen beings
the world insists UFO'd from Venus
but who, if the truth be told,
wear folded wings and broken halos.

Downed in a fierce dogfight
with scrambled Ohio flyboys over
Route 40 on their way to herald
Mary's next scheduled gig,
they prove the tight-minded folly
of those who, wide-eyed, live
to doubt. You don't buy it?

It's your funeral. Walk out
on a clear night. They light
every radar screen. Dominions,
Thrones in formation, bogeys,
pitchforks gleaming, at nine o'clock.
The Holy House flew all the way
from Nazareth to Loretto,

spinning like Dorothy's, to squish
the witch of our unimagining.
Heavenly beings rise and soar,
barrel-roll, peel off, stack up
over O'Hare and sometimes fall
to earth. Remember Joshua,
The Day the Earth Stood Still?

WALKING BY THE LION'S DEN ADULT THEATER AND BOOKSTORE, SISTER MARY APPASSIONATA EXPERIENCES THE STIGMATA

This thought like a red light,
gash of crimson salty as
fuming seas we struggled from:

loving ourselves, we bleed as one.
A baby wails in a mess of red;
we buy a washer and dryer

and live forever. Blame it
on the blood. One half
of all stigmatics are Italian,

Francis of Assisi the very first.
It could be—not a few
serious scientists claim—

that those operatically cursed
with the 5 puncture wounds
(read it and weep: 4 nails, 1 spear)

are bleeding hearts who think
themselves a drop too holy.
God dropped a heavy house on

Blessed Bloody Dodo of Frisia.
The *Dunstable Annals* tattle on
the man who nailed himself to a tree

at fairs, staining crowds below.
The Oxford Council staunched him.
He got life, a room with a pulse.

But blood's the wonder. Domenica
of Paradise ate only white wafers
twenty long years, although

she daily sparred with demons
and bled like a punch-drunk pug.
Francesca de Serrone's blood

stank of fresh violets and ran
hot enough to blister the fingers
of the hoo-hawing gawkers.

Walk into the furtive cinema
on Ladies' Night and watch
the paper bags and popcorn boxes

tick and throb in sparkling dark
in the laps of rapt believers,
god-smooth bodies on the screen

dancing, panting to raise a sweat,
and tell me love's not in the blood
and there's no miracle to us,

wounds to this flesh, no scarlet cord
binding together soul, mind
and the loud, travailing heart.

SISTER MARY APPASSIONATA ON THE CHOLESTEROL LEVELS OF THE GODS

They won't eat their vegetables.
Only Italian saints merit
pasta and polenta in paradise.
And how do you get a being
who's All-Everything to exercise?

In the Eumaeus of the *Odyssey*
after the boar is stunned
its bristles, bones, fat
and chine were barbecued
for Hermes and the Nymphs.

The gods lust for more
than one kind of sweet meat—
if you get my drift.
It's a wonder there are
leftovers for us mortals.

They like nothing better
than times of spitting fire,
the lean, bloody pious praying
loud over crackes of fat,
wreaths of greasy smoke.

Yahweh too liked his meat
charred and rare, tons
of roast bull and dove.
Also two-legged critters,
tribe upon wailing tribe.

Aztec Prime Rib of Human came
with tomatoes and peppers—
on a bed of gold maize,
for presentation. In time
we love every god to death.

Pythagoras, though he reverenced
everything alive, after
he'd discovered that the square
of the hypotenuse
of a right triangle

equals the sum of the square
of the other sides, axed
a hecatomb of oxen—
100 bawling, shitting beasts.
A fine mess we make of belief.

IV. THE WEIGHT OF THE HEART

NEANDERTHAL INVENTS PRAYER

Iraq, near the Turkish border
along the Zab, tributary
of the Tigris: Shanidar Cave.

Stone barracks for armed Kurds,
but only scratch the surface
of the bloody here and now

and sorrow grows timeless.
Workers stoop and rise, fall
deep into the Paleolithic.

Earth charred black as tar,
evidence of Neanderthal fires,
and eight arrays of bones,

a burial place, women and men
lying on the left side, biding
their time facing the fallen sun.

It will be eight years before
the story of this eternity
plays out, when back in the lab

the powder in the soil under
the new electron microscope
proves a more amazing find.

Arranged on the slide, grains
of pollen seem to float,
ghostly sex of wildflowers,

burial vault of hollyhocks
and a piece of butterfly wing.
Sixty thousand years ago,

a day between May and July,
the mountains shouting color,
the fluttering of wings light

as dawn-sweet mist, death
slipped into the cave with
its already familiar sting.

The tribe went out to gather—
perfect in their mortality—
these fragrant blossoms,

trying to staunch the night,
finality's sobering stench.
Neanderthals, our kin perhaps,

though it's easy for us
to dismiss these chinless ones—
ridged brows, heavy cranial vault—

as brutish cave-women, cave-men.
But one of them was the first
in the face of fear and awe

to dare to imagine *ever and ever,*
a life that smells like heaven,
our first prayers, the flowers.

ILLUSTRATION

. . . the skeleton of a British defender, Maiden
Castle, Dorset, who died in the Roman attack.
An iron arrowhead is fixed in the twelfth
thoracic vertebra. —Kanowski, *Old Bones*

From 43 A.D., Celtic designs
articulate the empire of ruin
when Vespasian's legionaries

breached the wall after long siege
and spelled their fury,
soil strewn with broken teeth.

In hurriedly-made graves,
34 skeletons, including 11 women—
some with hands still tied

behind their backs,
a restraint more horrible
even than death fixed them.

Most skeletons are young,
in their twenties and thirties,
the age of raising war and babies,

for it's the human way to send
young ones down the aisle
hand in hand, bound for both.

Shattered skulls moan out
the savagery, wounds
that bloomed at death-time,

textbook-perfect sword-swaths,
sliced limbs, jawbones
crushed, kicked clean away.

One young man lies here
still bent from the weight
of the barbed iron pain

that went in the front and stuck
fast in his backbone. I hear
the scream of his piercing.

When I was young enough
to believe, I was told that at
the Last Judgment my soul

would seek out and find
my body, which would be made
perfect as Eden before the apple—

the two to be reunited
to sing or burn God's pure mercy
forever and ever Amen.

And now I can almost feel
that in the tale this field tells
of the great chain of suffering

with which we bind one another
we can see something close
to the near-immortal soul

deep in stony bones, the place
of our most stubborn art,
bones that say and say our lives.

HOWARD CARTER UNWRAPS KING TUT; OR CURSE OF THE MUMMY'S TOMB

O Osiris, King Tutankhamun,
Your Soul is in your body eternally.

I made the find after tunneling
to the last wall. I noted
the eroded penis spindly
in its gold sheath, time
a more demanding lover
than any goddess or consort.
All around were figures
frozen on the wall.
I was learning to read.
After my stainless scalpel
eased through linen layers
stiff with unguent centuries
and found the faience of beaten gold,
royal diadem still bearing
its writhing cobra,
pectoral of all-protecting,
hawk-eyed Horus, I came upon
the real art: flesh and flowers,
history's ancient scents,
bone's brittle geometry.
The mummy's curse? To endure
this life almost forever,
and then the discovery,
dead self lost in living light.

ALABAMA FARMER JUST MISSES BEING
LAST CASUALTY OF CIVIL WAR

—Associated Press

The trash of war collects, ordnance
of each skirmish back to the first
arrayed in tiers beneath our days.
Flint-flaked axes and arrowheads
bear the stain of blood and scream,
brass buttons, tons of bone.
Walking even our greenest terrain
we dash our feet on ancient disputes,
bite lips to tongue the brackish froth
of the too-human taste, haste, hate.
On his John Deere, putting down
herbicide in a field of beans
the Jackson County farmer drove over
the pitted globe not much larger
than a child's skull, tossed it
in the toolbox and finished up
his rows. Explosives experts
from Ft. McClellan were called in
to detonate this precious heirloom,
a relic that tells us more
of what we are than any jawbone
unearthed from the Olduvai gorge
or elk leaping from cave wall:
bitter fruit from seed too often
gone bad, harvest
of a dark and random past.

BATHING LENIN

For the Hero of the Revolution,
bath time. Every year and a half
he's taken from the glass coffin
and reverently undressed.

They study each mole and wen,
the technicians, lower him
into the tub to soak a month
in a secret beauty fluid,

the achievement of Soviet science.
The West has nothing like it—
their leaders rot like offal
while Lenin's lips are supple.

Sensors, color monitors
stand guard. Nearby, a lounge
for the battalion of specialists,
white-coated Dr. Frankensteins

whose duty is to preserve the state
beyond its own decease, lave away
the least difference between this
and any living dictator.

The only change has been
to darken the hair a bit,
to make him seem more vigorous.
Seventy years of lying in state

for the saint of the state.
If conditions were maintained
he could stay on eternal display,
ultimate art of social realism.

But out in the republics
the very ground shakes
from thuds of marble heads,
torsos tumbling from pedestals,

tanks parading the pavement
to resurrected, ancient anthems.
A vivisection of power.
Whether he remains publicly dead

or enters earth will be,
as death and ever-after must,
purely a political decision.
There is talk of a vote.

The people wish to live.
The people want bread and meat.
The people are hungry enough to rise.
Everything changes

but the pink hollow body
without heart or brain
bobbing gently
in its warm, rippling bath.

SWASTIKA

Forestry officials in the town of Zernikow just found
a huge swastika-shaped patch of light-green larch
trees . . .   —Newsweek

Aloft, we can read this world,
decipher our mean designs,
the glyphs and lines
we use to force earth
to wear our small ideas.

Some evils are seasonal.
Spring, the larches hope
against darker evergreens;
fall, they hold day's gold
like trembling hands.

Planted fifty-two years ago
by a troop of Hitler Youth
stooping as one in cruel boots,
they grew, vicious whispers
outliving war, the camps.

Can we pretend we've grown
beyond silent greeds,
shrill unisons of tribe,
a forest shouting out
a sign more obscene than money?

The crippled cross can't be
cut down, for in absence
it would glow louder,
a cold hole in our days.
Only by clear-cutting

can perennial acres
of unspeakable ache be erased.

Should we once and for all
fall to work with chainsaw, ax,
tree by lovely tree? No.

This scar must be preserved,
a monument to our gift
for twisting blessings
into curse, the very trees
saying *Hate, hate, hate.*

THE SHINING PATH; OR, THE PSORIASIS OF ABIMAEL GUZMAN

From the Greek, "to have the itch,"
it's a chronic disease of the skin
marked by persistent inflammation
and white scaly patches.

It can be a terrible affliction.
It seemed you were evolving
back to plague-time, and farther,
to the slither and hiss we were.

How many of your fellow citizens,
weeping mothers and old ones
among them, did you march up
the Shining Path, *Sendero Luminoso,*

into the sun, Presidente Gonzalo?
25,000, I've heard. "The Fourth
Sword," they called you,
behind only Marx, Lenin, Mao.

It maddens! But you mustn't scratch.
It was to save your skin
you came down from the mountain,
seeking to shed the coat of fire

growing over your bones.
The lower altitudes, farther
from the sun and the rare air
of classroom idealism gone mad,

are not as dry. And here,
in the wealthy Lima suburb,
among the perfect lawns
of the bourgeoisie, the soldiers,

dressed as cable installers,
took you. You offered no resistance.
And would you even now think this
the very height of madness,

that after twelve years of scream,
the tiny teeth of children
glittering among shattered glass,
seeing you a sick frightened man

in a cage before the generals,
I can feel for you, the flesh
in its slow smokeless erosion,
the sores seeping, seeping out

the human pain of a brother?

WITH THE VISITING WRITER

For Aleksandar Hemon

He and the interpreter
sit across the table
at a Thai restaurant
in Columbus, Ohio.

He's a Croat; his father
came from the Ukraine.
I'm American; my family
fled Italy and Slovakia.

We laugh. Neither of us
knows the way home, he says.
Our pens are compass needles,
I say. And cocks,

he replies. We decide
we don't need the interpreter.
I say, this city is excited:
the year of Columbus,

Colombo, Colón—whatever
we call him. *D.P.,*
he says. We laugh again.
Your literature, he says.

Plath. Dickinson. Ginsberg.
We lift glasses of Thai beer
to Plath. First,
Slovenia raised the old flag,

he says. It alone
may survive—if Germany
doesn't eat us all again.
Young ones are fleeing.

Soon in all the world
Croatia will be the oldest—
older than Ireland.
I say, since Appomattox

we've not smelled war
in our kitchens.
Singed flesh mingling
with cabbage, he says.

I blame the Serbs
but centuries we got along.
It was in the blood.
Now we chew our babies.

Lovely Dubrovnik, Sarajevo—
dumps. The goddamn army
I blame. The blood's theirs.
Generals, politicians,

hooves and tusks stained
with shit and blood.
They failed at being communists
even. Then communism failed.

Now they say *Democracy*
and *Fatherland* with
the same piggy voices.
How can they not fail?

Exotic, this cuisine.
Lemon grass. Coconut milk.
The joy of everything other.
Bitter as tears, this tea.

EGYPTIAN TOMB PAINTING,
AZTEC SACRIFICE,
CENTRAL OHIO AUTOPSY

The Egyptians, loving their deaths,
slit open the dead and lifted out

the heart, its chambers quiet
finally as black rooms of rock

deep in the Valley of the Kings,
the last grave-robber scurrying

toward Thebes. Anubis the Jackal—
Thoth recording the results—

balanced the heart against Ma'at,
Feather of Truth, goddess of goodness.

The Aztec priest sliced the chest
deftly, grasped the pound of will

and thrust his red, pulsing hand
to heaven, food for Tezcatlipoca,

Mirror that Smokes, King of Gods.
In a bone-cold lab, the Deputy Coroner

of Franklin County studies the heart,
savior and betrayer, sweet, cruel heft,

to determine if any crime occurred
beyond the usual felony of desertion.

I think of my own drum-solo, intimate music,
life's rhythm shared only with those

who love me, those paid to keep me.
Feel me. Here it sounds; now it's still.

I'm now loud; now not at all. Systole,
diastole. A child, the wonders

I believed: that each sneeze, and later
each dire climax stopped the heart

an instant, the dark's feinting,
a temporary forever. In fits

and starts, dare and cease, coming
and going in wild cadences

against the feather of everything,
of nothing, loved ones taking sides

around the bed, each moment a judgment
for good or ill, I weigh the heart.

AFTERWORD

After it's all been said, what more needs to be? What can be? Presumably, a collection of poems ends as each poem does, in the margin, the white, pristine silence whence it all came. This page should be nothing, therefore. Absolutely nothing. The nothing which extends before and beyond and on either side (and even between the lines), the words which produce light and heat, motion and music, the poem in progress.

But for the reader who helps create the poem in the act of reading, life goes on; for this reader, in fact, the poem may well continue to happen in the mind after it ceases to be on the page. Nor does the poet, unless the act of creation was utterly overwhelming, lose consciousness at the poem's conclusion. The sound a poem has made can echo, fading into something whispering and insistent. The scent of a poem can remain on the hands, the lips. The images can be burned into the back of the eyelids, to bother our vision, trouble our sleep.

A poem can change a heart, a mind, a life, but these transformations happen only rarely. At the very least the poet can say, if all has gone well, that he or she has made progress in the saying, that the poems are "better" than the poems of the previous book, or at least that more things seemed possible to the poet in the attempting to say and the actual saying, and more still will be possible when next it's time to say—in poetry. Of course, for our purposes here, all this would be said in another language, in prose, that other, more public, less pure way of saying. And we know, from Robert Frost, what gets left out in the translation of poetry.

Actually, there are things that can be said. My sense of an "Afterword" suggests that brief section appended to a novel or other narrative work by which the author, in a kind of temporal shorthand, cheats time and breaks the frame, the "rules" of the story, by giving the reader a peek at the future of the major characters, as in, "Jason and Heather, perhaps because of the heart-wrenching and turbulent trials detailed above, remained wonderfully happy together (despite the fiery-eyed Raoul's return to Santa Nada after he'd served out his time in the state pen), producing 12 pretty children before they lay down side by side in the sod after deliriously happy deaths; and they remain at peace to this day."

It's only human to want to know what happened, at the end of course but even *beyond* the end. What is the eschatological working out of the tale after the tale has ended? The saying after the saying? What is the *after-word* beyond even *the word?*

The poems which precede this little essay are far closer to the lyric and meditative than to the narrative, but the poems are dramatic at the same time, often revealing moments of the lives of individuals, and it might be of interest to the reader to have a sense of what happened to the major characters, to learn how they turned out in the end (after the end, the last line of the poem in which they appeared).

The various fathers, mothers, daughters and sons in the collection continue, most of them, to do their best to know just what it is they're supposed to know and do in this life. Cleveland Stadium was replaced—for baseball only—by the new and lovely Jacobs Field. As I write this the Indians are acting like the best team in baseball, but none of their fans is getting his or her hopes up. California continues to rumble and shake its inhabitants. Calabria smells much the same as we can imagine it did in the time of Pythagoras, whose discoveries are no less important to us today than they were to his age. AIDS remains the horrible plague of our days, and our situation seems more and more dire as the disease devours its quota of our most talented and creative souls.

Our society being what it is, and our memory, not to mention our minds, more folks should be praying to St. Anthony, patron of lost objects, than ever before. Daisy and the other lost children remain in darkness, as does the nation of vagrants within our nation. The songs of Phil Ochs and Elvis live in my mind still today, years after the music ceased for each of them. JFK has suffered somewhat lately, but still his reputation places him higher in the estimation of the nation than Lyndon Johnson, or (certainly) Warren G. Harding.

Nolan Ryan has retired, to the delight of opposing batters. Although I've had to give up the faith of my childhood, I can't see a rose in its labyrinthine lushness, its dewy youth, without thinking of Therese of Liseux. The Lion's Den is closed periodically by the police and politically ambitious assistant prosecutors, but it remains a house of dreams and worship for countless lonely dreamers. The venerable Sister Mary Appassionata continues to pay visits to me, speaking her wild, fervent beliefs in ways that convince. Is there nothing she can't believe? Was I that way, once upon a time?

Nationally, cholesterol levels dip and rise—mostly rise. Hearts contract and swell. Neanderthals are enjoying a renaissance of sorts. They weren't nearly as dull and dense as we originally thought.

Lenin remains in a state of perfectly imperfect preservation, even as the nation he left behind falls farther into dissolution. (There is a rumor about that Disney wishes to buy the body.) Serb, Muslim and Croat continue to pray their hatreds to their gods for no other reason than that they have always done so. (We must admit they do it exceptionally well.) In the Valley of the Kings, over-digging, especially in the minor tombs, due to the desperate push of young archaeologists for academic tenure and promotion back home at their American universities, has threatened all the tombs with flooding and collapse. We still have trouble keeping our hands off the dead.

Anubis the Jackal and Ma'at, the Goddess of Truth (often represented in Egyptian funerary art as a feather) were right. Lighter and lighter our hearts can grow if we try (no matter how vain the attempt ultimately must be) to do no harm, to live the careful, considered, considerate life.

—The End (?)

To those I love
You know who you are

BARBARA D. HOLENDER

Is This The Way
To Athens?

BARBARA D. HOLENDER, a native and lifelong resident of Buffalo, New York, is the author of *Shivah Poems: Poems Of Mourning* (Andrew Mountain Press, 1986) and *Ladies Of Genesis* (Jewish Women's Resource Center, 1991). Her poetry has appeared in numerous journals and anthologies, most recently *The Helicon Nine Reader* (Helicon Nine Editions, 1990), *Scarecrow Poetry* (Ashland Poetry Press, 1994), and *Lifecycles* (Jewish Lights, 1994). She was educated at Cornell University and The University of Buffalo (B.A. '48). She is a lover of music and languages and is presently engaged in intensive Hebrew studies.

CONTENTS

ON THE WAY TO ATHENS

EVEN TO BEGIN

The performer's nightmare,
said my teacher, is to forget
even how to begin;

wherefore she nerved us
in recital with the name
of the first note.

In daymares now
committed to perform
unable even to begin
we wait in the wings of our lives
certain if someone would only
whisper the first word
we should know how to go on.

THE LITTLE LIFE

My luck is such
that during the Golden Age of Pericles
I would have lived in Spain.

I am that Zen goose
in the famous unbreakable bottle
no exercise of wit will get me out of
but that I squeeze back in, saying
politely, Is this the way to Athens?

Still, even the little life
is susceptible to greatness—
sometimes—within—
a dislocation Plato might have felt

when like a Chinese bridge from fog to fog
rises a thought
that holds our weight.

A FIELD OF GREEN TABLES

My mind spreads in the old books
like a foot in a worn shoe,
easing into impressions
I first sized up as a schoolgirl:

of Dickens—a winter apple,
of Chaucer—rich sun on coarse woolens,
of Milton—a pillar of fog,
of Shakespeare—a field of green tables
for attics of critics.

A taste of questions (a question of taste?)
survives as an ought of response
not to be breached by reading Dickens in summer
or coming to Shakespeare wholly for pleasure.

Yet, as returning to a once-known room
one leans against presumably a wall
turned door, the too-familiar mind
fixed on some yielding phrase is hurled
into a world of thought unthought before,
and wakes astonished as Miranda
to see the people in it.

THE LISTENER AS PERFORMER

(with the Guarneri Quartet)

Seated onstage in the sold-out hall
we resonate to the swoop and soar
of the notes flung over their shoulders.

I weave the rhythms with my flexible foot,
a boy's boots bounce in counterpoint,
the lady on my right affirms the themes,
especially the cello's, while the fellow opposite
chins himself on the upbeats

as Beethoven flashes like St. Elmo's fire
from the bowtips.

They could do without us
but here we are, joining the struts and ties
till our bright edifice is shattered by applause

and, spent with making, we too
beat the broken air.

BURCHFIELD PAINTS A BIRCH FIELD

The skin of the trees stands on edge
Bees tense
Flowers importuned by giant butterflies
cave in.
        Reach out—
you are in this picture.
What you have said to the trees
is about to happen.
The flowers are a case of nerves.

The thoughts of the trees
speak through your hands.
The trees are painting
this picture.

I. *Body Parts Italiano*

On the day of the prophetic rising
in this marmoreal boneyard
faces will find their noses,
castrati their private parts,
gesturing hands their fingers;
torsos, heads, arms, feet will assemble
in a danse macabre, clicking together
seamlessly. Rome will be built in a day,
Firenze overpopulated, tourists discomfited
by white staring crowds.
Ah, they will say, recognizing
an eloquent shoulder, a fabled decapitato,
this is all very fine,
but is it Art?

II. *A View from Below of Michelangelo*

In the museums of Florence—
a parade of penises in various moods,
some assertive, some askew,
some vandalized down to the pendant plums.

We see after all that these,
especially in marble, are embellishments.
A doctor observes that the genitalia of David
are too small for the rest of him.
All binoculars focus. He was a kid,
says the guide. Persists the doctor,
Also his nipples are too far apart.

The women adorned with knobs or globes
cover their lowers with hands
or draperies, or close their thighs
lest one display a cleft of rose
or apple split.

He liked the boys,
yet these are no oriental excitations
but simple renderings, homo erectus
leafed and fruited, so much lovelier
in polished stone than all the maidens
mute with Freudian envy.

III. *After Hours in the Sculpture Gallery*
(Borghese Museum, Rome)

As the visitors leave, Pauline Bonaparte Borghese
rubs the stiff elbow she's been leaning on,
munches the pale apple, and sheds the draperies
from her lustrous loins. Time for a little diversion,
but no prospects in sight, save David in the next room,
snarling at an invisible giant and stretching his sling.
Good bones he has, and sinews, very sexy in his anger.
Aeneas, on the other hand, is sensitive
but overly occupied. Perhaps he could unshoulder
the burden of his father, prop him against a tree,
the Daphne tree there, partly leafed already.
Actually, Apollo's the ideal catch, on the rebound.
Pauline muses on an arrangement of Anchises
and his dutiful son against a leg of Daphne,
and draws Apollo onto her gilded couch.
Go to hell, he snaps, unreconciled to his foliate fate.
Whereupon Pauline slithers into the Great Hall
under the eye of Hades bearing the weeping Persephone.
Can't stand women crying, he mutters, and sets her down
to get over it, leaving Cerberus to guard her
with his three toothy maws. Persephone rubs her leg
where Hades' fingers have dug deep. Around the room,
ancestral heads stare from their pedestals.
She feels their disapproval, but Pauline,
entwining arms with Hades, twitches her white hips
at all those bodiless boys.

Yiddish poem
your bones stick through your borrowed clothes.
Poor immigrant
your relatives are always explaining you
while your displaced persona
cries out in its own voice
"That's not what I said!"

How anemic you are.
Back in the old country
your blood sang like wine.

You speak to me
of lost family connections
but in this exchange
I am the poor relation.

BIBLE STUDENTS IN THE SUKKAH

What does it matter
that we are forever looking things up
and forgetting them?
Our minds are like the sukkah:
crowned with evergreen
open to the stars and winds
hung with our best fruits
and reconstructed each year.

The pine boughs shake down sun,
the leaves of our books cast up light,
and all our ancestors
cluster around us, saying
This is who we were
and *this* is what we did
and *this* is what it meant.

So it must have been at Pumbedita
in ample Babylon
where our Talmudic fathers
from every jot and tittle
extracted meanings
and over golden dates and wine
discoursed on the family tree

and one always had a story,
and one always said, Be serious.

WAY STATIONS

AMONG THESE ROCKS

My eyes burn with staring bare at the sky
from the floor of the gorge, and my throat's dry.
My pockets sag with stones, and my thumbs itch
from the grain of ancient granite, quartz and flint.
A few immortal leaves are cast in shale,
the shaftless arrowhead no longer wounds,
and everywhere the sense of having been
informs these walls like an old anonymous genie
wanting out.
                    Nature's peculiar thrift
has made a monument of the unwanted,
reducing history to hieroglyph
and science to surmise.
                    If I turned fossil
among these rocks, geologists would note
the attitude and date the armature,
but who'd know that the eye sockets streamed with wonders,
or that the brain pan brimmed with names of things,
or that the strange striation of the bone
was the reaching strain of a city girl
encompassing a country day?

CLOUD COVER

Watching the underside of
what flying over
the upper side of
resembles snow-skimming

I am reminded that
there is properly no up or down
in space; there is only in or out.

Looking out, then,
from my precarious chair,
in seeming less secure
than *down* I am aware

those icebergs bloom and break
across a blue deep danger,

and I have vertigo
adrift aground.

—No comment—said the president
of the Flat Earth Society,
confronted by earth's curvature
as photographed from outer space.
(Note that he did not recant.)

—The fact is—they told him . . .
No facts, please,
we all have facts. What people want
are meaningful measurements, such as
up is good and down is bad
and left is wrong. That's what a man
gauges his life by. Earth's all edges,
precipices, crevices,
and we have fears of falling.

Sometimes in nightmares, I inhabit
a ball hung whirling in a void.
I cling like down on a dandelion,
knowing that one good puff. . . ! and watch
everyone trying to get off.
Or worse, I wake in fear the world's
the shape we act as if it were:
a box within a box within
a box within, all opening in.

Fact is a chosen image from
the angle of your preference.
Near ground, where I fix my lens,
Round does not photograph. Round is
the verb "to know" intensified.
Round is Now, caught like a breath
till your ears pop and your eyes swim,
and a long exhalation turns
earth over into time.

CRUISING GLACIER BAY

After a week of our grumbling at the rain,
the sun splitting the morning fog
kept the captain's promise.

At the head of the bay they waited, glittering
rivers of ice. Silence was the right response.
LOOK! we shouted. And the glaciers calved,
great icebergs tearing away with a roar and a hiss.
Blue sky, blue ice, blue sea, festooned with clouds,
and I with only two eyes to take it in
and a lens to diminish the sight.
All I wanted was a place to stand alone
watching the drowned clouds swallow the sun
and the mountains brood over the glacier beds.

There's a row of heads at the bottom of my snapshot—
nowhere could I perch above the crowd.
I scaled the ship that day for solitude;
now for company I plumb this photograph
for a familiar scarf or hat,
the recognizable back of a head.

SALMON RUN

Salmon coupling trouble the shore waters
of the bay, thrashing and leaping clear,
eluding eagles and fishermen.
They have breasted the ocean
to fling themselves upon the falls,
rise to the river, against all laws
of physics, straight up, returning
to the beds they left as fingerlings.

They are frenzied, desperate to be done,
yet it's not the exertion of the run
but the change from salt to fresh
that rots their living flesh
pale rose, translucent silver.
Toward the sweet death is their desire,
a closure brief and brilliant, seed spawned,
all uses spent, and disembodiment.

THE TEMPO OF POSEIDON

The strident voice of our Greek guide
stomps out every syllable:
THIS IS THE MAR-BO TEM-PO OF PO-SEI-DON.

I drift away from the harsh lecture
into the surreal light of Sounion.
The tempo of Poseidon is molto largo e calma,
the air suspended, the paper ships
stuck to the horizon.
Everything waits for Theseus.

Later, bathing below, we look up
at the slim pillars of everlasting grief,
and speculate on the angle at which Aegeus leapt
into the sea, and whether he took a running start.

The black sail hovers in the distance,
lads and maidens saved to dance
upon a vase; the votive fire, extinguished,
revives in the strange anticipatory light.

Micini, the scullery maid, shakes down her hair,
ties a towel around her hips, and sways,
transformed, to the bleat of the portable radio.
The captain has found anchorage safe
from Aegean winds, and the crew motors ashore
with bread and olives, cucumbers, tomatoes,
bottles of ouzo, retsina, beer.
The goat they told us was a lamb turns on the spit;
Micini's hips flick like the flames,
and the beat of her tough bare feet
echoes the smack, smack of fresh-caught octopus
tenderized against the rocks.

Salt rimes the swimmers' limbs and lips;
in a cloud of ouzo, the sun drops
through a slot in the mountains. Torches flare,
and now Micini turns on the captain's arm,
while the best dancer of the crew dips and leaps,
slapping his sandy soles with his palms.
Upa! upa! we cry. The waves slap the shore,
and the moon dips and leaps from sea to sky.

LA FÊTE CHAMPÊTRE

But I can't speak French, I say in French.
Oh but you must, they say.

So in this Monet garden, under a dappling tree,
a small breeze sighing Debussy,
the poulet grillé laid out
like an odalisque on its bed of greens
with the perfumery of wine and mangoes;
to the delicate click of cutlery
and the howl of a hound on the tail
of an hysterical mallard,

in an eloquence of eyebrow, shoulder,
and interpretive fingers, I who cannot speak French
speak French, and Agnes who cannot speak English
speaks English and Kandace and Genevieve speak both
and the dog speaks dog, and the duck gets away.

The point is, I read somewhere,
if you don't know a word, make it up;
nine times out of ten you'll be right.

Such a lovely pique-nique.

THE TANK

(Kibbutz Gonen, Israel)

Two were captured from the Syrians.
No trophies, said the government, seizing one.
The other, hidden under brush,
became a plaything for the children,
first generation to grow up above ground.

Disarmed, disemboweled,
painted in pastel camouflage,
it blended into the garden.

Give back the gun, said the children,
not to be pacified with less
than the genuine, but quite content
that it sat harmless as a pied bullfrog
among the blossoms.

The dark magic
that turned children into moles
in subterranean playrooms
could make it bloom again
with fire.

Caperbushes sprout through dry crevices, spattering shade
on stone, eighty feet above the congregation.

One chassid among the flock of crows—that one—
dances with himself in prayer,
sways left, now right seven times,
forward thirteen, now seventeen short bows,
again and again, pliant as a lulav,
his shadow advancing, earlocks matching
flying curl for curl, even the fringes
of his tallit, almost even the stripes
sharp in shadow, so clear the light,
so light the air, ah that Jerusalem air.

At almost sunset, the students explode
four, six abreast, in a running dance
down the Yeshivah staircase,
across the square singing, singing,
echoes on echoes, so many students,
now single file, hand on shoulder
each of the one ahead, round and round;
the songs rebound from the golden wall
as the Sabbath descends.

The caperbush sways in the moonlight
against stones moist with supplication;
zmirot, songs of Shabbat, float
over the square, shalom, Shabbat shalom.

From the shadows beyond the wall,
the muezzin's hoarse cry.

ENCOUNTERS

HAPPY BIRTHDAY BUCKMINSTER FULLER

(Chautauqua NY 1979)

On his 84th birthday he climbed on a chair
assembled his toys
and, head above the audience,
turned the structure of the universe
inside out.

I am desperate for time, he said,
I have so much to tell you;
and he nimbly flipped
a tetrahedron, octahedron, icosahedron,
and twelve spheres around a central sphere.

The crowd ate it up. The universe
grew dense, packed with his energy.
Not a scrap of space was left.
All structure comes to this, he said,
the four faces of a tetrahedron
never let you down.

We took his word for it,
having no better metaphor
than the universe as old man
happily juggling
under that great geodesic dome
in the sky.

RUNNING

As she speaks, I see the flagpole falling
where she stands paralyzed
while they shout *Run! Run!*
I hear the crack of her spine,
feel the weight of the pole, the lifting,
the numbness. All in her voice,
twenty years after.

It is still happening
as she tells it, her hands
gripping the wheels of her chair;

still almost not happening,
the voices in her shouting
and she running, running.

HEAD OF A YOUTH

(*Los Angeles River*)

They found him in a snarl of brush,
still mouthing O—
a flotsam kid swept from his bike
no-hands all that long way.

Once it might have seemed a great adventure
to go floating down the river like Huck Finn,
under bridges, past waving crowds,
the fire department hollering from the shore.

But the flood rushed down
at 35 miles an hour
and there was no raft

and the crowds threw ropes
and the fire department launched a boat
and the helicopters tracked him
as everyone yelled encouragement—
and once he shouted back—
and the TV camera showed us
a head, sailing past at 35 mph.

No one, no one could stop him
though they hung from bridges
and checked their watches downstream
as if they had an appointment
to meet just here, just now

until the water and the head
went down, somewhere
they hadn't looked.

PLAYING BINGO

I want to bury him back home, she says,
so I've got his ashes in a beautiful container—
not one of those pots—more like a book
with his name engraved on the cover;
and he's settin' right on my dresser
and I talk to him all the time.
Does that sound crazy to you?
Not really, I say.

Well, she goes on, last night
my friend called to see how I was, and I says,
Fine; we're just settin' here playin' bingo.
And she says, Who is?
and I says, Why me and Sissy and Bud.
And she says, What're you talking about,

Bud's dead, isn't he?
And I says, Well yes, but he's right here
with us at the table in his little box.
And she kinda choked and said real fast,
Well take care now, bye.

Do *you* think I'm crazy?
Depends, I say, who won.

THE WIDOWS OF CORNWALL

Door to door they go
the fisherwomen
to every house in the village
Over and over they tell
how their men were lost at sea

At every door they keen
the same raw strain
till everyone believes
till everyone can say
So that's what happened
Ahhh

That is their custom
Door to door they go
telling and retelling

Then they go home
and tell themselves

METAL MAN

My friend says she can't sell her house
because she has 37 barrels of silver ash
in the basement. Her husband's a metal man.

If I had 37 barrels of silver ash
I'd have a metal man too. I'd
melt it down, fuse it, form it
all shining rippling muscles,
gleaming chest and thighs, and I'd put
a silver tongue in his mouth.

And when he touched me
I'd turn silver too, glisten
like a fish, a mermaid, so quick—
silver—Oh

STRAW INTO GOLD

(*A Middle Age Romance*)

She can do it herself—
with no dwarf's magic—
out of her straw heart,
her dry belly, her dusty mouth.
She will tell you a grandmother's tale—
a phenomenon—how the mere wisp of love,
not even a touch, the thought of a touch
spins gold finer than any maiden's
and worth the price.

Down her limbs, out her fingertips,
up through her scalp, she pulls
each bright nerve from its sheath.

Round and round she spins,
gold heaps about her
weaving a shimmering skin.
She is drawn through a needle's eye
tight as a caught breath
waiting for the good gray king
to gird his courage on
and plunge his heart
into her burning breast.

THE LITTLE MERMAID

You're all torso and tail, they said,
how can you win a human prince?
I loved him enough
to try being human myself
though my godmother said I must walk on knives for it.
Very well, I said, watching my tail
turn into the train of a gown
and my feet dance out from under.
No one told me how to get the knives to my feet,
so I swallowed them.
It was hard going all the way down
but I felt truly human
with my slashed insides and my dancing toes.
When the prince married the princess after all
I walked into the kitchen
and laid myself open.
They found my pure white flesh
featherboned with little blades
and my tail like the train of a gown
and they heaved me back into the sea.

They're raising my statue on the shore gazing out;
I can't imagine what she's looking for.

COLLAGE

She is a cutout
on an endless frieze.
Frayed shadows mark
where she no longer fits
against a torn background
mired in thick impasto.

She carries her small gray shape
as if there were a place for it,
a space exactly matching her contours
in a scene lacking only her form,
a harmonious landscape in which
she provides just the right note—
a picnic in the open air, perhaps,
with a welcoming crowd
and one anonymous face
that has been waiting for her
all this time.

SALT

For all I know,
it may be Lot's wife, said my friend,
handing me a chunk of salt
from the Dead Sea. It looked
like the arch of a foot,
a fist of someone my size.

I saw her, treading
the thin crust of virtue
day by day, step by step,

brimstone seething below,
not daring to glance aside
or hope for relief.

Only when the place blew up
and she was spared
could she stop and turn and see
the landscape of her life laid out.

Old tears, pooled
from foot to throat,
clogged all vessels,
every aperture.

I licked the stone.
What my tongue learned
took all these years to tell.

SPEAKING IN TONGUES

(Ulpan Akiva Netanya, Israel)

I. Learning the Language

One day in Bible study
Clarence is asked to read text
in English. He starts, hesitates.
What's happening? He's American,
surely he can read English.
He smiles sheepishly—
I started reading from right to left,
he says, It made no sense at all.

* * *

Where did you learn Hebrew?
I ask Armenian Inessa.
Here at Ulpan, she says.

And where did you learn English?
I don't know English.
Suddenly I realize, all along
we have been speaking Hebrew.

* * *

Akiva, an illiterate shepherd,
began to study at forty,
became a famous rabbi, a scholar.

Smaller than any of my classmates,
I tower above them in age.
Every day I learn, every other
day I forget, in and out, in and out.
They help me, these bright youngsters
from Russia, Germany, America,
and I brood on them, how hard
it is to be twenty.

Barbara is the "ima," the mother
of the class, says Charlie in Hebrew.
She has "nisayon." What's that?
Life experience, he says wistfully.

II. *No Words*

> *for Faina Volotyin,*
> *who cannot read this*

So, if you could tell me just one thing
in this new language, what would it be?
That we have come from earth's far ends
to meet by chance? That you
who lived from hand to mouth
live now from mouth to hand?

Our tongues are the tongues of children
in our philosophic heads.
Rich thoughts shine in our eyes
like gold in a shop window
just beyond reach. We shrug,
spread our fingers, smile helplessly,
riffling through our dictionaries.
Each day a little more—ten words, twenty—
we can reveal ourselves. Too soon,
too soon I return to my life, you
to yours. We clasp hands, lock eyes.
In all our untranslatable ways
and last in this shared tongue, we say
Ein milim, ein milim
"There are no words."

III. *Sing Shabbat Sing Shalom*

Someone has picked mint for this tea,
followed her nose in the dark.
We sip and sing in the courtyard;
stars big as plums hang
in the listening trees, the moon
climbs the scale of one pure voice.
Whoever knows, sings in Hebrew.
Who doesn't, hums along. Now
the rhythms change—Arabic lilts
from our reticent friends.
We clap the beat, we la la la.

If it were up to us
we would launch songs across the borders,
big balloons of words like the comic strips.
What do the songs say? Love, mostly.
And longing. There are in Hebrew
five words for longing, four for peace.

BLOODLINES

"My brother Sam played the violin," said Tante.
"Once he broke a string, but he went on playing,
and then another string broke and he kept playing,
and then another one broke and he ended up
playing on one string. With nine brothers and sisters,
you can imagine how much laughter there was in the house."

I remember my grandparents' holiday table,
lined with aunts and uncles, studded with cousins.
It stretched from the kitchen wall through the sun room,
and there was a separate table for the littlest ones.
There were two Uncle Sams, one by marriage.
Both played the fiddle, but real uncle sang Peezie Weezie,
and marriage Sam sang Abdul The Bulbul Ameer,
and his face got very red.
For years we all sang in that house.

Then one string broke, then another.
Alone now, but for one untuned completely,
Tante plays the last remaining string.
"Somewhere," she says, "I see them all,
and as each one leaves this world, the others move over
to make room." Her ageless face shines
in anticipation of an endless family meal.

UNCLE CHARLIE

At seven forty-five a.m.
at Delaware and Lexington
his heart said "Stop."
His hands went up
his life flew out.

Strangers he would never meet
who clocked themselves by Charlie's feet
still waved at windows as he fell.

Small comfort to his wife to tell
how neatly he had taken leave.
It was the rush of relatives
that kept mortality at bay
and stuffed the cracks with "Charlie'd say."

For those who set their lives by his
and matched his wit and kept his pace
the days went slack, the years grew taut

and once the mainspring had been caught
his aging siblings knew, too soon
who'd marched them up would march them down.

You don't have to answer every crazy thing he says,
I tell my cousin. Whereupon her father fixes me
with a fishy eye and, suddenly recalling my name,
invites me into the kitchen for a drink of water.

You have thirty minutes, he whispers mysteriously.
Behind his stare I see the nerves
waving like sea grasses,
reaching out across the failed synapses.

We are each other's favorites; he would tell me
if he could. Telepathically
I try to bring him back, take him back:
Uncle the sportsman, sharing his catch,
hat bristling with lures, pail brimming with bass,
and all of us kids eating fish, fish, fish.
Uncle the sport, with his fine suede jackets,
his mid-parted hair and teeth, his cheerleader laugh,
embarrassed tears, incomprehensible party song:
Mushadingaya, faddladdla, my son Miggie,
mushadingaya.

Now his mind is parted, and his lure
is toward his dead wife. He tells his son,
I want to die; you're a doctor, help me.
He flounders, thrashes restlessly
on an endless lifeline, while his daughter,
her heart flooding over and over, is quietly drowning.

I. *Preminiscences*

They are looking into the mouth of death, my parents,
not a reliable ventricle between them,
and eating life like a picnic.
In our weekly long-distance calls
they giggle like kids
telling me what they've done.

We're a little frail, she says,
warning me; *We're on a slender thread.*
This is a new tone. Always
she has said, *Fine, dear,*
in that voice to which the only right response is,
Come on, Mother, what's the matter?
Now I say, *If I can't fix it*
I don't want to know about it.
And she laughs.

Two images possess me:

> I am taking my first steps,
> each hand in one of theirs.
> My father has a special name for me
> that no one else will ever speak.

> They are walking away from me
> hand in hand, and not turning back.
> She is unafraid, he's
> wistful and a little scared,
> but keeping his spirits up.

Trying to loosen my grasp,
I write the final pages
as if I could avoid living them,
spare them pain

and send them together
like good children
timely to sleep.

II. *My Mother's Monument*

The column of my mother's memories
is engraved like the Rosetta Stone
with every injustice ever done her.
She deciphers them for me: This one

used to be my friend
but she took up with that one
who did such a thing to me,
so we aren't friends any more. And this one . . .

Mother, I say, how can you carry such a weight?
I'd fall over. But it is her ballast.
Though it shifts with her embattled loyalties,
it validates her choices.
I know my friends, she says.

When somewhere dark in me, remembered evils
swell like mushrooms, I have little taste for them.
She savors like a salt lick
her unrelenting core.
I know my enemies, she says.

III. *My Mother At Prayer*

She goes wigless only before God.
On the edge of her bed,
fine hair scarcely covering her scalp,
face unlined at eighty-three,
trusting to wake or not to wake
at peace, she talks to Him.

They have been friends since once
He almost took her, and changed His mind,
to spare her for my father.

I recall in less precarious times
the tartness of her ridicule:
No one of intelligence believes
in a personal God.
Now she wakes in gratitude
sounding like her mother:
Thank God, another day.

You know, I have a very bad heart, she tells me.
No, I say, you have a very good heart,
only it doesn't work so well.

IV. *My Father Under The Oxygen Mask Took Hold*

The taxi arrived for me
at the same moment the paramedics arrived
for him. I want you to leave, he gasped.

Sure, I said, right now I'm leaving the country.

At eight we called the family. At ten,
the doctor asked if we wanted heroic measures.

At two, he struggled to tell me something.
Don't, I thought. Don't say goodbye.
I leaned closer. Pay the rent, he wheezed.
Tell Mom, it's the first of the month.

At three the doctor gave him, maybe, six months.
At four my uncle choked back tears:
Hey, you owe me two cents.
I'm broke, said my father.
Loan me two cents so I can pay you.

The day we brought him home
he recited a birthday verse
he'd written for me years before,
full of our secret Latin fooling.
It ended with "Amatus you,"
which he wasn't sure was right.
It's perfect, I said. Amatus you, too.

Eight months later, on their sixtieth wedding day,
he said to his bride, We made it!
The family came from all directions.

In four weeks we were back. The day he died,
my uncle gave my mother two cents.

V. *More Air*

Her chest squeals like a well-chain
as she delves deeper and deeper
to haul up each bucket of breath.

Amazing, she says, I wouldn't expect
any piece of equipment in my house,
even my house, to last eighty-seven years,
and I'm still going, of course
my arteries are shut, they couldn't get a tube
to my heart, but I'm doing the best I can.

While the pump heaves, the chain creaks,
the days suck air from her lungs,
I worry about hospitals, worry
about nurses, worry about money,
dutiful daughter-machine,

and I say to the mother-machine
in the mirror, No, no,
I am my father's daughter.

VI. *God's Gentleman*

I wear his battered hat, his bolo tie.
The family album shows my eyes
and mouth are his; his are my crooked fingers
tracing the spidery script of his last letter—
Dearest No. 1 child . . .

God's gentleman, the rabbi called him,
and quick-witted, a caring man
whose outer and inner selves were one.
The whole congregation saw me nodding, smiling,
as the words gave my father back to me.

In his name, a Biblical garden
blooms in Arizona. I see my creators
in the cool of the day, walking to and fro.
My father bends to console my mother.
Me, too, I say.

VII. *My Mother Courting Death*

My father never rejected her before
he slipped off alone at dawn,
not saying, See you later, or
I'll be back to get you,
though she knew he would, knew
he was somewhere around, reminding her
to lock the door, finding her car keys.
She waited for years, never shed a tear,
thought he squeezed her hand
when she sang their old songs.
But he, who was never late for anything,
didn't come and didn't come.

Having no lover, she chose Death,
courting him as wantonly as a proper lady could.

She reached for his hand, he pulled it away,
gave him her heart in a quivery box,
he sent it back postpaid.
Once in desperation she walked right up
and stuck her head into his big mouth.
He spat it out.

When Death finally waggled his finger,
she dropped everything and set off
without even her house key.
Halfway there, three quarters, almost there,
someone blew the whistle, called the medics.
With a laying on of hands and electric shocks
they turned her around, tied her hands and feet,
gave her a shove and said, Run.

What could she do
but make the long journey back,
start over waiting waiting waiting,
singing the old songs,
wondering when her number would come up,
why her first love had forgotten it,
whether indeed she even had one.

Remarkable, she told her children,
I was really dead and they brought me back.

And who among us is most broken-hearted?

VIII. *Lantana*

So many years
my visits have begun
with the story of lantana—
Imagine, from one little plant
its roots underspread the entire garden,

and its tendrils crept
and bushed and choked all other growth,
until my father, cutting cruelly back,
unwittingly renewed its vigor.

Now my father is cut down
and we, rooted in love,
talk and talk of him;
our thoughts tumble and twine—
enlarging, embellishing—
choke out his underspreading absence

as through me echoes like a mantra,
lantana, lantana.

IX. *Facing the End*

Life, the rabbi said, is the shadow
of a bird in flight. The bird flies away,
the bird is gone, the shadow is gone.

Mother, wings spread, you wait,
the greeting grown stale upon your lips.
Death does not oblige.
There's nothing left of me, you wail,
it's all gone, I'm nothing.
No, I say, surprising both of us,
it's all here, in me.

At once your whole life's energy
informs my blood, that woman bond.
How much I bear of you who bore me,
standing in the shadow of your flight,
imprinted with your bright trajectory.

THE BRIDEGROOM

for Fred

A rooster out of Chagall, you strut
down the aisle. Under the canopy
you crow your vows.

Your bride fades out mid-phrase
till you remind her where she is.
Her name is Barbara, like mine.

This is my wedding. It will be years
till you are born, and grow old enough
to visit my Chagalls in the gallery.

From the upside-down house
in your favorite painting
peers an old woman. Is it me?

But I am in this wedding,
where a bride of my name
takes a man of my child's name

while the bird cries Ready? Ready!
and the wedding music flies out
the primary-colored windows

and your father's eyes say,
The house *is* upside down
and we are aging backward, love.

A GIFT OF GALTONIA PRINCEPS

for Judy

You would have managed to meet at least
the Chairman of the English Department
or the visiting dignitaries
if not the President of the College,
instead of a gardener eight-months homesick for England—
not the Director of Horticulture
but the prospective Head Gardener of the Lilies;

would have brought home a contract or a contact
instead of a damp pocketful
of chive-like *galtonia princeps*
that come up lilies
and which are so expensive it's a shame to waste them,
lucky I came by.

Then I was too dirty to meet
the President of the College
or the visiting dignitaries
or even the Chairman of the English Department;
and now I have let it out
that the Head Gardener of the Lilies
has given away expensive seedlings
to casual visitors.

Well, I was not casual.
All day I sat under the scholar tree
whose compound-leafy branches end in wisps
like metaphysical thoughts,
and traced the Mill River
orderly as a curriculum,
thinking at random.

How selective random is.
Watching the pleasure birds and the business birds—
the acrobats and those that fly for transportation—
framing the mountain half in half out of the river,
and the wind's thumbprints on the water
shored by yellow birches coining a new season,
I tried to imagine chaos.

All I brought home
was a sense of form and a bag of sprouts
I didn't even plant,
knowing nothing grows for me but in my head.

Now in November's early killing snow
in that way you call disorganized
and I spontaneous
September's onions
come up lilies.

FOR MY GRANDSON

Bone of my bone
Flesh of my flesh,
Teething Sam gnaws my finger.

Child, I am mostly gristle.
Such nourishment as you can get
From me, you're welcome to.

But I am fed from you
As from the springs of Engedi,
Where little goats

Leap delicately
Over the ancient stones
On sharp-toothed hooves.

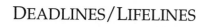

DEADLINES/LIFELINES

THE CUTTING EDGE

for my father

Faster than the pronged stars in flight
is the distancing of death.

As the padded days wear thin
and the watch-candle gutters out
comes a wild moment of freedom
just this side of desolation
when the living are honed
to the last enduring nerve.

Severed clean as with a blade
the planes of being
shift.

DEADLINE

A line where the dead cross
over, that edge of the mind
where the living, reaching out
strike air

a fence the dead peer through
whispering unintelligible news
of where they are

a tripwire dead ahead
where the sea leaves off
and the world falls away
Here be dragons

dybbuks[*] breaking in, Listen, will you
never listen, never? until
the line goes dead.

* Dybbuks: spirits of the dead that possess the bodies of the living

MY DEATH

Every day it misses me
on the highway—
Not yet.

Every day I miss
the skate on the stair,
the bone in the fish—
Not yet.

Maybe it is augmenting me
like coral
or a more vegetable growth.

It whistles through my teeth,
I sway on my stalk of life—

Not yet.

TALKING TO A DEAD MAN

Four years later you come barging in
as if you still owned the place,
never noticing that I am weary
and wish not to be reminded,
and that with grace and care
I have pearled a new shell.

This hole in my life is not for filling,
it's for cautious circumventing.
Drowned there, you rise to my gaze,
and I push you under.

Will you never be exorcised?
"Only tramps pierce their ears."
I did it, bought colored stockings,
reset my wedding ring;
still you abide with me.

When I feel most myself,
I open my mouth and you come out—
the flesh made word.
Shreds of you hang on—
I remember the shape of your teeth,
and forget your smile.
Did you ever live? When did you live?

Ah, now that you've left me alone—
leave me alone.

I saw him standing across the river,
his face clouded, angry.
What could I say?
I don't want to think of you
because I am happy.
You are too young for me now.

Suddenly he was at my side,
his hand extended. We kissed—
not kissed, exactly, but found ourselves
in the middle of kissing,
sucked under, our mouths one mouth.
I did not breathe,
then I breathed water; I pulled,
but could not pull away.
Pushing with all my strength
against his shoulders,
I burst upward, throat streaming.

He is gone down again.
My lips ache. Six years
they have touched nothing
but my teeth.

YELLING AT THE DEAD

They are never still.

Bury them, they shake
the ground beneath your feet

Seal them in a vault,
they pound on the wall

Scatter them, they swirl
ashes in your teeth.

They sneak in,
steal your thoughts,
twist them around.

Keep yelling,
make them answer
something you can live with.

THE PALM TREE

Fifty years later they found him
murdered, old soldier spy—
Bedouins pointed out the "Jew's Grave"—
under a tall palm, his skeleton
entwined with its roots, sprung
from the dates in his pocket.

I always thought
I'd meet world's end
with a song on a high branch.

O Lord, let my heart take root,
let my bones arch upward,
let small birds sing in me.

Young women in the shower room
nubile bodies bending,
stretching, breasts and bellies,
buttocks, thighs taut and tender,
pliant as willow withes
you towel and buff.

You do not hear me singing
under my breath—
Oh, if you only knew
I am one of you.
My markings are the flow
lines of the tides; inside
I'm firm as an apple.

Once I kissed a prince
into a frog. He cursed me.
Entranced by your eloquent
young men who come
borrowing coffee, admire
your shining floating hair,
whisper Diamonds are forever,

I wait for my last chance boy
rising from the sea
shriveled and scaled
to gather my rosebuds
while he may.

GLEANING BUCKEYES

Pay no attention to this gray-haired woman
kicking around under the chestnut trees,
smash, bend, scoop. She has been gleaning buckeyes
fifty years from these same trees, on this
same campus, sorting the squirrels' leavings,
stomping them from their burrs.
How they gleam, the good grain spreading
from the stem-scars five, six shades of wood.
Don't eat them, you'll die.

Never mind the children are long grown,
the grandsons past these outings.
She is the schoolgirl, ever Octobering,
glossing her harvest with remembering thumbs.
But whose crabbed hands are these
cramming the pockets of her life?

SONG FOR HER NEXT AGE

Ride, ride old woman
ride down your days, hound them to heel
wind in your teeth, ride to the sea
salt on your tongue, brine in your blood
naked and nerved, sing down your days.

Howl down the sea, old woman
into its mouth cry out your name
into its wake cast off your bones
into its womb bury your own.

Old woman, rise from the sea undone—
you have won, you have won.

Afterword

I have been on the way to Athens for a very long time, so long that I have begun to realize I will never get there. I did go to Delphi once, and all the way up on the bus I thought of the ancients toiling up that precipitous path, only to be rewarded with the mystic equivalent of the "glowing rejections" I've had all these years. It probably didn't matter; the ascent was the important thing.

I've written poetry since grammar school days, mystifying myself and my family. It just came out, and my work all these years has been the long process of learning my craft. When Ted Weiss asked if I wrote only short poems, I replied that I'm a peripatetic poet; I write on my long walks or over the laundry or in the shower. Put me at a typewriter, I freeze. Set me under a tree by a lake and the words pour out. Short poems are portable, shorthand is fast and fluid, but print is committed— to be avoided until I'm sure I really have a poem.

Many years ago when I was one long exposed nerve, writing how it felt to feel the way I felt, I wrote a personal poem, not confessional but not obtuse. Reading it to a friend I said, I think you're thinking you can see my bellybutton. No, she said, I'm thinking you can see mine. That was my liberation, and the materials of my life began to make poetry. I have tried to tell the truth, as Emily Dickinson put it—but "slant," which happens merely by selecting which truth to tell. I've had the good fortune to be around some wonderfully quotable people, and my quotes are real.

This book has been many years in the making. I'm happy that some of the old poems lasted and seem at home with the newer ones. Somehow out of it all came the shape of a life.

MARIA BANUS

Across Bucharest After Rain

*Translated
from the Romanian
by Diana Der-Hovanessian
and Mary Mattfield*

MARIA BANUS is the leading woman poet of Romania. Published when she was only 14, she created a literary sensation with her first book and her work has continued to grow through periods of war, occupation by Nazis and by Communists. She has been praised and translated by leading European and South American poets, including Pablo Neruda. Many poems have appeared in English translations, but this is her first book in the U.S.

DIANA DER-HOVANESSIAN, the author of 13 books of poetry and translations, won the Van der Bovencamp and Armand Erp award from the Columbia University Translation Center for *Land of Fire*, selected poems of Eghishe Charents, as well as PEN/Translation Center fellowships, and poetry prizes including NEA and Fulbright fellowships. MARY MATTFIELD, a poet and translator from Romance languages, was professor of world literature at the University of Southern Massachusetts.

CONTENTS

ACROSS BUCHAREST AFTER RAIN

LETTER

Sssh. I am writing to you because
tonight is a night like the brow of a faun,
because the roof of my mouth is as bitter
as the thin skin of green walnuts,

I am writing to you because both of us
are so forgetful. I am sure
we will forget even the pale
flutter of our eyelids soon.

Remember. We were walking. Suddenly
my tousled hair fell over my face.
The wind gusted. Treetops shriveled with dust
and reached for each other with a soft rustle.

There was acacia. There was also the sea.
We had stopped so I could shake sand from my sandals.
That is all. Your ankles were dearer to me
than heaven and earth.

SEPTEMBER

Jeweled September. The stork rests on the chimney.
The garden flaunts new colors—
silvery purple satin on the cabbage,
velvety red tomatoes, colors weavers envy.

In the kitchen plum juice is bubbling.
Fuchsias dust the threshold with gold pollen.
And the young girl sitting there to read
drifts across her childhood.

MY ANCESTORS

My ancestors,
workers of metal, shoemakers, tailors
craftsmen in ancient towns,
humble craftsmen in the old ghettoes,
famous craftsmen on the principal avenue
craftsmen on their knees,
beards torn out,
tongues twisted,
craftsmen from peaceful towns
with heavy bronze bells,
with parades of flowers,
and newborns swept off by fire and sword,
the threshold shadowed,
the terrible days on guard, the festival days. . . .
My old craftsmen, scattered
from one horizon to the other,
sleeping under the walls
of stepmother cities,
my old dead,
how you were humiliated by others,
how very much you feared others.
At night, I too, I hear
that crazy squeaking. . . .
A little peddler
is crossing the wood
that links one village to the next.
And night has fallen.
Such apparitions in the wood,
a hand, another hand,
two eyes,
a gliding step,
an abyss . . .

And beginning again,
the claws and the hands,
the eyes and the breathing,

the hissing, the mobs
of people, of people.
That shrieking of wheels,
the cart that runs madly
through the forest of people.
And the peddler cries, Flowered scarves!
Glass beads! Mufflers! Shawls!

Out of the deepest sleep
a tormented fistful of clay
howls and falls back.

SEPARATION

My name washed off
and waded across the water
to the other side of the ford

through the autumn wind
through the flood of leaves
we can scarcely hear each other

I catch sight of it
looking me up and down
from the other bank
with a guilty ironic smile

while I make myself
smaller and smaller
curling up, forehead on knees
in autumn's womb

YOUR NAME

I have forgotten everything, stranger.
Even your name has blurred to a tuft
of cotton, a fluff of lichen on bark.

I used to open the telephone directory.
(Isn't it strange there were telephones
then? So many thousands of years
seem to have gone by.) The pages were lined
with dull, dead names which I climbed
toward yours, as if to a funeral pyre,
toward the core of fire, toward the logs
made of incandescent syllables
ready to surround me with their swords of white heat.

Or in passing, someone would speak
your name. Some fool who would throw,
without knowing what he did, the switch
unleashing a current of thousands of volts;
which would immediately start another torment,
another transport by fire.

A slender filament would light
up in the slightest object,
even the table legs, the window sash,
the picture and its frame,
the handles of the fruit bowl
lit into flaming spirals of
long neon snakes flashing on,
flashing off
at night, on movie marquees.

Then those in the room would notice
that your name instead of dying away
in the air, like all the others, was building
up as lightning does. They would stare,
their eyes turned into carnivorous

beacons curious to spy out and track
the underground passages,
the secret recesses where your name advanced
like a river of lava.
I would have nothing left
for covering myself, nothing
for defending myself,
as the beams burned
and my damp hair stuck
to my nape and temples.
The hunting, ravenous look
rummaged into the most hidden
corner of earliest childhood,
into the holy arabesques
of spiders' webs,
with stones, flowers, beasts,
with names forbidden to all.
I stayed stock still,
uncovered, in that world,
without defense, without hiding,
without running.
All perspective had vanished.
I was an old primitive painting
with reality and mystery in the foreground.
I see myself as it was,
motionless, cheeks flaming
among the transfigured objects,
which the slender white hot thread
of your name was passing through,
your name, stranger, your name.

NOT BY DESIGN

You pull this way, I push that.
You, all frantic flood,
I, logic, static and sad.

What an unlikely pair, O God.
How unnatural, even obscene
this coupling of horror and farce.

But yet, how splendidly
the pieces, the details,
of this demented art fit.

DIE REICHES—KANZLEI

There are no military sentinels
at the gates.
There are no gates.
There are no eagles
and no swastikas on the walls.
There are no walls.
There are no spittoons
nor armchairs in the rooms.
There are no telephones.
There is a gray fine rain.
And concrete. A few gray slabs.
And in the cracks of concrete
blades of grass and chamomile.

There is no longer anyone
in the Chancellery.
Only the rat.
The rat of the earth
has remained

and he runs,
gray and fat.
Self important,
he runs through the bunkers
and the stalls
and makes telephone calls,
makes telephone calls.

GEMÜTLICH

Gemütlich, the German word
translated, flickers and fades.
Pleasant? Familiar? Easy? Agreeable?
No. In German it has a different shade.

Gemütlich has cottage curtains, flowers,
napkins edged in lace.
The tick-tock of an old clock,
coffee klatsches in a cozy place.

Gemütlich after a brisk walk
through wind and fog
finds you at home in your
castle with your dog.

They gave you orders you obeyed.
Canary, dog, wife, are still.
You are the master here,
and you relax to pay your bills.

Gemütlich—the little graveyard
on the hill
with angels, and old willows
all sun-filled.

You listen to the ticking clock.
The nearby marketstalls
are being taken down.
Twilight falls.

I travel through one
German town and then the rest
and think of Germans lost
who sleep east and west

under strange skies, vanished,
crushed, where they went.
Over their graves foreign winds
and bitter mint.

They sleep badly under cold clods
in an unsheltered place
with no canary nearby
no curtain made of lace.

They went to distant places.
They ordered. They obeyed.
They killed. And they sleep
in the bed they made.

Gemütlich—a kind of painting
on pottery cups and plates.
Light flickers on the pitchers,
on the window panes and grate.

A woman grinds the coffee.
The clock strikes. Tall
shadows pass in the white enamel,
bloodied shadows, one and all.

So much time has passed since
I saw you last. I was afraid
you would not invite me again
to sit in the garden arbor
listening to the dripping
of the fountain.
I was afraid you would not invite me
back to my favorite place
in the alternating shade and sun
of the vines. I was afraid,
with the quaint folly of age,
that I would be attracted
toward the mouth
of the cellar and I had convinced
myself you would drag me down
to where slugs and spiders,
stacks of damp wood, rusty
basins abandoned by women
and babies, to where worm-eaten
vegetables, wrecked tables whose
last supper trickled down
into the ground.

I knew that all I had to do
was descend a single step
to glimpse another open black mouth
leading down into another yet deeper
cellar crammed with darker things
that have lost their meaning,
battered kettles, decaying leather,
unraveling embroidery, a dead grand-
father clock with obscene
weights dragging time to lower depths.

I was afraid you would hold my thin,
aging hand in yours with the iron
vigor of folly.
Still I am bold enough
to walk right into your yard.
Everything is proceeding according
to my imagining.
The only surprise is the intensity
of the blackness whirling deep
into itself in the black holes
as I step behind you
groping down the walls
trying to cling to brackish
green slime.

There are recesses at each level
that get warmer, steamier
and unbearable as we descend into
the endlessness of black and slime green

and then black and green and green
as we reverse and ascend
toward green
air, green water, green
unripe grapes under
the green arbor.

Out of meaninglessness I breathe
meaning. I quaff
the vine's breath.
I breathe in and out with the house,
dog at my knees, fawning.
We talk again
in the light,
me with words, you with your eyes.

When I pass through these streets
of my old Bucharest I summon
and sometimes even bring to life,
yes, revive for a fraction of a second,
the inexpressible state, the fusion
of self and things:
the restless shadow of chestnut trees
and the dazzle of glazed verandah
spread like a peacock
in the drowsiness of noon.
A little pink plaster gnome
peeks out between the flower
beds of a lawn, all the shivering
play of shadow and light,
all the inexplicable arrangements
of the city: porches
and porticoes of inns, absurd Moorish
villas, low houses
in courtyards with fountain and
narrow wooden walks,
shade of the trellis
where suspected guilty loves
hide, the cool chambers
redolent of mold and quinces
(jam jars with sticky lids,
great stags racing on the wall hangings)
and the street vendors,
the chained watchdogs asleep,
and the lords of the old palace
themselves steeped in indolent nostalgia.

I feel that inexpressible state of being
detach itself from me
not violently like a bandage yanked off
but one without haste, unfelt, almost
gently.

It is the work of time, I tell myself,
calm and treacherous time,
dismembering me delicately
bit by bit.
But at the same moment I am that child
again as I stretch
out a leg completely straight ahead,
teeth clenched, while my mother
in front of me sponges my knee
with warm water, and it is true,
there was no need for fear.
Lightly the gauze bandage lifts off
without pain. It comes unstuck
from the wound and the horror
with which I stare at the live flesh
drains away. Everything comes free,
everything, without pain.

THE MONSTERS

The sideboard is huge with belly and paws.
And how dark it is!
It wears a notched wooden crown
like the fairy tale Black King.
And opposite is the wife of Black King,
the sofa with its bolster
and padded back. She also wears
a little crown over the worn velvet.

They left me alone tonight
turning the key.
"Papa is beating Mama," I murmur
a funny song. From close by I make out
words like grubby scum of stifled tears.
And the monsters with paws watch me.
It has become dark.

Like small phantom fishbones,
like silver nerves
in transparent leaves,
like the tiny clavicles of an elf,
this day of carved ivory,
of carnival beauty
tries to fool me but cannot.
I know you, you charmer.
I know by the cast-off shell
of the decaying crayfish
guzzled down to the groin.
No matter how many disguises,
I recognize you, my lord.
I feel your breath
fanning my face
like white, like ivory,
like silver webs of a spider
and I want to be buried
in a magician's arms.
I can touch you, my lord.

GAMES

Goblins snatch the plate
right out of my hand,
pull the stool out from under me,
and laugh at the fun it will be
when the old woman falls head over heels.

Whom shall I rant and rave to?
Innocent little things,
cruel, in green leaf tunics,
they blend with the foliage,
their tasseled caps
have been ruffled and dampened
by streams, no, floods.
Oh, imps, stay a little longer.
Tease a little longer.
Don't vanish into the torment-free,
hoax-free night.

AT THE END

My lord,
you are far away
but your arms
have grown so long,
so long,
that when you swing me
you are holding me
from far away.
You hold me
and swing me
slowly
so slowly
from so far that
colors blend,
get so mixed up
I no longer know
when the light goes out
from its shell
and when it comes back.

BROKEN

Why are you surprised?
It is only a bone
of one finger
trying to play notes
along the keys
of leper piano
eaten away from within
and you are amazed
that the old glory
of Ave Maria is not
wrapping you up to
rock on her lap.

TIME

Madam,
unclench your fists.
Comrade,
clench your fist.
He's coming and
there's nothing
you can do about it.
He is advancing slowly.
And, yes, I am walking
toward him beneath
the wide, luxuriant
angles of cranes flying
through October velvet.
My fingers stiffen
but I lean gently
forward
then, lean
on the shoulder
of my beloved
assassin.

NAKED

My lord of a thousand faces,
actor, morris dancer,
how you caper, jingle bells
on ankle and wrist.
How quickly you change costumes,
contours, make-up and lines

Your red and blues are magnets
for me, your swoop and whoop,
your cries thrill me like love.

Hey, where is your make-up,
your motley, your tunic?
Why are you naked like a baby
at the beach? My lord,
you show me a pale face,
skin stretched over clean bone,
and gaze right through me to the sea.

THIRD EYE

I lost a stocking
and wept
in frustration.
I lost a glove and I cried.

I lost my left eye,
my middle eye,
my upper eye
and laughed so hard
I could have died.

BETWEEN TWO RUINS

Between two ruins
I built a house.
Between two treasons
I planted trust.
Between two chasms
I set the table
with napkins, silver and salt.
Between two mountains of corpses
I found a crocus that made me smile.
And that was my life. Can you understand
that is how I lived?

THROUGH THE TIDE

April's two legs
are chopped off
and every toe
every bud still aches
as if still there.

April knows they are gone
and hops along on stumps
through the high tide
of grass.

AT THE HAIRDRESSER'S

This cosmos has its own
snow of talcum powder
drifting from soft brushes,
and minute, rustless
spangles in effulgent light.
Everywhere—a small, appeasing hum,
an electric snoring of a tame
panther asleep under
rainbow enameled light.
A hive of honeycombs buzzes
behind protecting mirrors
and the jingle of coins at
the cash register cannot be heard.

Rows of mirrors yawn
and swallow more rows of mirrors:
a vertiginous point runs
to the infinite angle
where the scene is reflected.
As if through reversed binoculars

you see lines of women
under drying hoods
with loose capes under their necks
their faces basking in the light
like sunflowers, or long rows
of Egyptian friezes
with blind eyes waiting
for the radiant angel, time.

Yes, there are couples who make it to the grave
together like double yoked eggs in one shell
Victim/heroes of sleeping pills? Or cowards?

Should we praise them? Blame them?
Or let the city tribunals of justice pass down
verdicts after the usual balancing act?

This is the edge, the frontier now.
We have arrived, old things,
without planning to, on this
rickety wild race horse.

And all we can see from where
we stand on this bald plain
is an empty skull.

Wouldn't it be better now, old thing,
to look away? We have gone far,
too far. We might as well turn home.

And light the incense censors
and swing them left and right.
And in the smoke make jokes
and exchange bits of wit.
Let us blot out what is right
before our noses.

And let's say, for a laugh,
good, we'll die and then decide.

I SAY TO THE PENCIL

I say to the pencil
come this way,
the grass is soft by moonlight,
the leaves murmur like pigeons . . .
Cursed wretch.
It is useless to speak to you.
Where are you going?
Into gloomy courtyards
with scorched grass,
toward leaden bandages,
among rubble
and garbage cans.
What are you listening for?
There's a death rattle
at the back door . . .
Come away, I tell you.
No one can help them.
Good for nothing, do you hear me?

PREJUDICE

It's just an innocent prejudice;
everyone is entitled to one.
Mine is but a stray lily
in a field of sophisticated
theories on art. A daisy at an orgy.

It's a game, of course,
and I am playing with
crooked bricks. That's what I
was given for this game and
I have to use a mortar of dried blood
and mud. And so I build.
What? you ask.

Oh, it's a tower
with claws and beak.
Will it hold?
Will it stand?
Well, is there a plumb line,
a law, a nerve,
a tear at the end.
A heavy soggy tear
made of lead?

SONG CRUSHED BY TANKS

Do you think history can be revised?
Do you think history dies?
I praise what I loved and sing
more strongly than in the time
before tanks.

The rips, the gaps, the tears
of the wounded earth cry out.
And in the stained glass panes
the shattered face shines again.

ACROSS BUCHAREST AFTER THE RAIN

Perhaps this is the hour, this is the moment
when all my old cells have died
(once every seven years, they say)
and when the new ones are newborn, buds,
taking their first steps with me in the light
of the chestnut trees.
This June afternoon is made of pink and gray
strips of sky and watered silk
asphalt under drenched sunlit leaves.
How have I deserved, how can I pay for this hour of grace?
Perhaps with the years spent among the moths of my writing,
perhaps with the shadow of the scaffold,
perhaps with the ashen tint of my smile.
But how could anyone pay for this living virgin rose
in the flamingo colored hour, in the annunciation
of the chestnut trees?

CLOTHING

Some clothes, give me some clothes
for this thing.
Some old and beautiful clothing
to cover this thing, the nothingness of terror.
Take them from the chest of drawers
of childhood, or the closet, the wardrobe
of the great theater, angels' costumes.
You remember the one who comes in April
with a willow wand in his hand
who wears vast floating sleeves
that cover the emptiness of the terrible.

VACATION

I have not learned to live yet.
I dream at night of a blackboard
covered with confused fractions.
I tremble in front of it,
the chalk useless in my hand.
Do I know anything? Have I forgotten it all?
Here is the test to take again
face to face with destiny. . . .
But vacation is bringing back
the buzz of sunlight in the bending
branches of apple trees.
Vacation, by slight of hand, makes
the grass appear, and
with its motherly fingers
lifts the burden from my shoulder,
nourishing me, like a newborn,
with a drop of honey and
a pitying crystal sky.

THE NEW NOTEBOOK

Full of superstitions
I am beginning a new notebook,
white pages, sea spray.
Eyes closed, I am waiting
for moist lipped Aphrodite,
tresses in rose flames,
on the first day of the world
on her open scallop shell,
shy and sure of herself
as she rises from the salt,
from the primordial cells.

I wait behind closed eyelids
and under a low sky.
There is a gray murmur of gulls,
the monotonous shock of waves,
nothing but waves coming
and going.

THE INVADERS

Wordless, silent, masked
the army advances faraway
close at hand   in the distance

They approach, neither men
nor women but shapeless
voiceless demons

sent from hell to haunt
this territory
to throttle words in the throat
and scatter the treasury.

How can I defend myself?
Complaints and laments
my only weapon, my only shield.

Wait. Their silence wavers,
quavers, jostles into words
that seem to implore

something to stay.

It is hell they address.

DISPLACEMENT

If you are going to praise sedatives
praise valium too
it sweeps off
ghosts of the mind
it deflates specters of fear
it dissolves red rags stained
in the latest massacre
in the field choking with dust
something is moving
lapping holy water
from a chained tin cup
take a valium
flowers bloom
through the noon-heated
porch-slats sweet pea fuchsia
the dog barks in the distance
at the far end of the village
guarding the patriarchal gate
Is it the same cur
guarding the gates of hell?

PATIO

    Simple non-prescription
    drugs, easily come by
    in the pharmacy,
    say an aspirin
    might help
    to turn the night
    into an old patio
    by moonlight
    and there in the middle
    of the lawn
    those two
    counterpointed by the pillars
    will stop, walk on
    stop
    leaning together like
    two columns of air

DAIMON

    I know you are there
    nearby
    I saw you coming down the street
    looking great
    in blue jeans and checkered shirt
    you've brightened up
    the season of pale snow
    you demand extreme colors
    you act furious
    you shout: Either-Or!
    you bang my broken-down
    door with your fist

please knock
next door
they might open
for you

PIETÀ

What is this stretched across my lap?
The light is treacherous and I cannot tell
if it is a baby or an old man.
Is his flesh apple blossom or
shriveled dry? I cannot see.

I have no fingers now to feel
and let me know. Only my nose
smells life and blood.

The light is treacherous
I cannot know
if Calvary is moving toward him
like rising water, unstoppable,
or has it passed

wrapping him in tears and leaving
him on my knees?

CHOICE

You have two choices.
Either you wind your watch
say Good Afternoon!
It's Getting Dark
and watch Yorick and Ophelia.

Or you are Yorick and Ophelia.
Hamlet too.

And then perhaps
you become your own
symbol
maybe with a few warts
but you affirm
your presence for another day
half a day
half a minute.

THE CYCLE

First I learned everything
quite well:
numbers, names for objects,
places.

Then I rested
like the village idiot
staring and found

I have forgotten everything.

A cavern yawns in front of me
and I go down a step,
cross a lawn.
I graze like a horse.
I am a lamb discovering grass.

I go down another step
and find clammy roots
of trees.
Another step and the stones.
Light vibrates and I sit
to begin to learn
from the other side.

LULLABY FOR MY KNEES

Don't cry, knees. Don't stiffen and stop.
I will lead you like two lambs through
the fern and rain and night.

We will go together toward those iron knees.
Don't fear if they hold
you prisoner and press too tight

under the heavy astrakhan of dark.
The fireflies of the Steppes will dim
their glow. But the dark will end.

Don't worry, knees. I will help you bend.

LOST CHILD

What have I done, Lord,
to deserve this great fright-
ful dream. I am forty
but still a child.

I wake and
the blind filters in light
of morning. I am seventy.
Ecstasy. Simple, humble delight.

THE ARENA

I play with words. Sometimes with rhyme.
Exorcising demons, visions,
masks that threaten, ghosts from limbo,
ugly grimaces, mad alphabets. Forget them.

A god decays. It is out of doors.
I am dizzy. I am queasy.
And I stagger. I play. The same role.
The ring is empty. Nuclear age.

Will she climb into the arena? Plunge
into nameless spaces?
I persist. I go on playing. As if there were a world
of overly beautiful gods, of magnificent waves.

A SPRING FRAGMENT

A street where I pass, shoulders drooping
under spring weather cumbersome as a buffalo.
The paving stones and the stars
stay so well behaved they could be counted.
Only my song is tearing my dress
under that spring, which is as heavy
as the belly of a buffalo.

I stammer. And I am silent. Should I wait
among the hedges until the lilacs turn blue?
Behind my knees the flesh is as moist as a split apple.
And the whites of my eyes are clouded.
I am thinking as I continue like this, shoulders stooped,
of that spring, wistful and bare as the neck of a boy.

Everything was an enclosure,
shadow and sunlight;
everything was intertwined
like a wooden summerhouse
with slatted blinds.
The hand was beckoning.
Mysteriously
the strange object
came closer
trembling,
almost real.
Once again through the delicate branches
it was hard to distinguish what it was.
Only fate,
all around,
under the pale sky,
springlike,
only fate.

And now autumn is here.
Such a free autumn,
dancing with men,
dancing with the wind.
The doors open inward.
The voices come from within
and return.

APRIL

Harmony has arrived here with age
and accepting that I anticipate
its coming, knowing there will be no rage,
but tender gentility in our embrace.

Why should I wake the savage clash
of cymbals, stir the harsh discords of youth?
Wiser now we drink of aged wines, truth,
and pleasures that are calm not rash.

Ours, the multi-colored autumn, vast
dominion of leaves; their monotone shades past.
Ours, the cool and fragrant cellar's repast.

But what is this anxious shiver that warns
that April, that wild king, comes
to shatter and surround this classic calm?

Whenever the gulls fly low, before rain,
the sea invites me
to become a child again,
to go with it
as water, air, space, teardrop,
unspotted time.

How was it, Lord, how was it,
when I was a child, and
puzzled before this water,
full of melancholy?

How was it she used to come
with her light step
in dainty buttoned boots
at the hour of grace?

She would draw near
and the light feather
in her broad-brimmed hat
would brush my cheek
as she bent over me.

How quickly she passes close to me.
Hampered by her long skirts,
how soon she's gone toward the cliff
where no doubt someone waits.

Her slim hand, gloved,
I cannot touch at all,
and the trembling plume
of her shady hat
no longer kisses my cheek.

What they like best,
better than anything else,
when they are at table
with their guests
is to talk
of normal times.

They dip pieces of bread
into sauce.
They smile at the memory
and repeat
n o r m a l   t i m e s
with normal white bread,
normal games
normal crimes. . . .

I, with my napkin knotted
around my neck,
seated at the little table
doze
and see ostrich eggs,
white, oval,
n o r m a l   t i m e s
and the brooding row
of huge birds
grotesque and unreal
in the shifting sand.

Saying I am not afraid anymore
I look at the signboards, houses, grass.
And the magic of distancing begins—
the spyglass in which
at the other end
very tiny dolls
are playing mama and papa,
playing master and servant,
playing soldiers;
bang, one falls down,
not a trace of blood;
bang, bang, bang,
the dolls tumble over,
little tenpins
without a trace of blood.

I am not afraid anymore, I say,
I am not afraid anymore.

What's that noise? Papa? Gul-gul, gul-gul.
No. Gul-gul. Mama.
Sealed as snails are sealed. The key in the lock.
But beyond the wall some unknown sound
big and oily, coming with the tread of a seal
dancing. Oh, Mama, no, you shouldn't have. . . .
you shouldn't have come back.
I'll stop screaming. I'll stop bumping
into everything like a dizzy five year old.
I won't bite your cheek as if it were an apple.
I won't jingle like copper scarabs.
Don't come. Don't come near enough to see me.
I'm just as sticky and old
as you now, like a sponge or a cave
with a brook running through it, a brook
coming from the womb of time
looking for a way out into light.
It trails along making me understand
though no one is near to tell me
its name. Or what it is.
I don't understand why my eyes close.
And again I see our old wardrobe
with its blurry mirror
and my hand rising slowly
to hang earrings on a pale
shadowy large ear.
I weigh the ear down with heavy
red cherries. The hand is still
translucent. The mica stove
translucent like
butterflies seen against sunlight.
Once in awhile something shudders.
The hand. The flames. In a harsh tone
I say: I am five.
Don't let me ever forget . . . I must
never forget anything here.

The faded gas jet. The red velvet cover
on the table. Mama's sewing basket
left behind. Spools of thread.
A collar made of vaporous veiling.
A pincushion standing, quills upright
like a hedgehog.
Swans gliding on the firescreen
of the fireplace. White as ghosts.
The door. And outside
putrid water running.
And murmuring voices
in the harsh whispers of death.
And inside me a trickle
of gentle blood threading
its way into my narrow child's chest
and into my temples,
into my flimsy child's arms
while my brain tells me
I'm grown up. I'm five.
And crying won't do any good.
Anymore. And I know that nothing
sadder will every happen
no matter what.

POGROM

We are all sitting down for supper.
That's how the memory returns to me,
a silent lunar meal surrounded
by my entire family.

Then a visitor arrives through mists.
Even the unborn baby shudders, aware.
The rest of us gaze at our plates
while the spoons sing a strange air,

a song of fear and hatred, a song
of evil spells and dread.
We take the food to our mouths;
he spins his black thread.

Then the executioner spider
slides down the web.
Silver glints on the table.
Our ears tingle disquieted.

With a hot iron the executioner
brands our foreheads with death
while Mother urges: Eat! Eat!
And we hold our breath.

The spoons carrying the message
sing the only song of revolt,
and the baby in the womb
grows wary and old.

PSEUDO-PSALM

Lord, my Lord, I pray,
what will become of us?
We are nothing but layers
of clothes, layers of skin,
like onions.
In a dry autumn,
in the stripping away,
I peel off, cast off
dry bandages in vain.
Under them I search
in vain and find
only skin and more skins,
pale, scorching layers.
There's no bulb, no heart,
not in the ground, not in the wind.
I am, 1 was only skin.

ALONE

My mouth is full. I cannot shout.
I've sunk my teeth into a crimson crescent
of watermelon. Why not? Did you think
I would wait for a dinner bell to invite me?
Shining seeds and ripe pulp trickle down
my chin.

My ears burn, my face is a mess, but I laugh.
If I stand on my toes I can grab the moon
by the back of its neck, by its downy nape
and send it spinning along the fence.

Tonight I'll knock on all the closed doors
with my fist, while my old nostalgias chase
themselves on all fours to bring back
the smell of dust, of man, of firewood.

Light shines on my forehead like sweat;
I wipe it off with the back of my hand.
I blink. I laugh at it all, everything,
while something swells like the sea
and lies heavy between my breasts.

ANGEL OF DEATH

One day the angel of death visited,
disguised as a baker, white flour
on his hands, his face, his clothes.
A sweet fragrance of bread emanated
from his oven, bread baked in light.
In beautiful rhythmic rotation
like the sun and the moon, round loaf
after round loaf went in and out.

"I am not afraid of you, baker man.
Don't you look just like old Ianni?
Yes, from my childhood street,
from that paradise of pastry shops."

This is just what I was saying to him
when he turned his face toward me,
a face bathed in hideous light,
and roaring behind him the ovens
of the holocaust, and I saw below
his flour-dusted apron how the good
baker, the angel of death, had
a trunk growing into the earth
covered with poisonous mushrooms
clinging to, growing on the roots.

LATE LOVE

I knew this was coming
this hazy land
but what surprised me
was all this ectoplasm
wrapped in misty shrouds

And the two of us still
hand in hand with all
the old discarded words

and between the words
invading our nostrils
a scent of blood

from the land of heat
from the land of scuffling
and we too still hand in hand.

GEOLOGY

was a slice of buttered bread
eaten in the school yard
a slice of motionless clouds
in a photograph
a slice of shriek drowned
by words, the fragrance of pines
thinning out into words,
layers, sedimentary schists,
my mountain.

AGORAPHOBIA

All right, then, stay at home
I said to the frightened fluttering
soul which resembled a plucked chicken,
with burned tufts of feathers sticking out
here and there, a scrawny neck, its eye
making a purple round in its socket
as it fixes on one point.

All right, stay at home, I said,
if you are frightened of the square,
the cars with wolves' eyes glittering
in long ever-moving rows.

Stay at home if you don't
trust traffic rules.
If you feel the back of your head
bearing the weight or being crushed
by steel girders. If you hear
the cracking of bones under metal
dinosaurs their claws and muzzles
stained by the puzzled blood
of the storied pedestrian.

Go home, Psyche. Even if
there is no home, no porch,
no turret, no window sill
where your soul can lean
looking down watching
the way young ladies of olden
days watched pageants,
ceremonies in courtyards
markets gallows,
watch the procession
of buffoons in fools' caps
who panicked at runaway horses
while buffoons whined and yelped.

There was no place to hide.

AFTERWORD

Born in 1914, Romania's best known woman poet, Maria Banus, has survived censors, pogroms, and dictatorships. Despite them, she has written some of the most tender love poems of youth, some of the strongest poems of old age, as well as political poems disguised as dream-like episodes.

"Thank you, Maria Banus!" Pablo Neruda, translating her work into Spanish, wrote in 1957. "Thank you for the steadfast throb of your love and dreams, for your magic web whose threads of smoke and gold draw in, from the depths, so many grave memories, like fish from the ocean, nets that capture the wildest butterfly of the Romanian plains."

Neruda understood how those wild butterflies skimmed a dark political landscape. Her poems, surreal yet personal, jolting yet beautiful, were mysterious enough to pass by Ceaucescu's censors.

Her first poem was published at 14 by the greatest contemporary Romanian poet of the time, Tudor Arghesi, in his review *Bilete de Papagal*. Her first collection of poems, *Land of Young Girls*, was a great critical and popular success.

The French critic George Emmanuel Clancier has said, "Her lyricism is not limited to language. The poet does not divide herself from the moralist. In a unique ellipse she brings beauty and tragedy together. Rarely are books capable of offering us at the heart of the poem such a union of strength and sensibility, of grace and tension."

Alain Bosquet puts her in the company of Anna Akhmatova, Else Lasker-Schuler, and Gabriella Mistral. "If we review three of the greatest figures of the kind of poetry which is lived in the very fibers of the flesh, we see that Maria Banus reaches the same height and breadth as these three. She is of the same race. She embodies better than any other writer the vibrant truth and glory of an age in which nothing remains constant. And she tells love as few women have known how… " Or men, we could add.

—Diana Der-Hovanessian

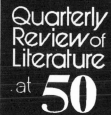